That's Funny, You Don't Look Like A Teacher!

That's Funny, You Don't Look Like A Teacher!
Interrogating Images and Identity in Popular Culture

Sandra Weber and Claudia Mitchell

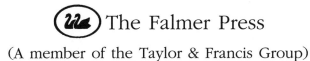 The Falmer Press

(A member of the Taylor & Francis Group)
London • Washington, D.C.

UK   The Falmer Press, 4 John Street, London WC1N 2ET
USA   The Falmer Press, Taylor & Francis Inc., 1900 Frost Road, Suite 101,
        Bristol, PA 19007

First published in 1995

**A catalogue record for this book is available from the British
Library**

**Library of Congress Cataloging-in-Publication Data are
available on request**

ISBN 0 7507 0412 8 cased
ISBN 0 7507 0413 6 paper

Jacket design by Caroline Archer
Painting by Deirdre Mackay

Typeset in 10/12pt Garamond and printed by
Graphicraft Typesetters Ltd., Hong Kong.

Contents

List of Colour Plates

List of Figures

Acknowledgments

Writing an acknowledgment is a challenge indeed. How to adequately express the fine quality of the many contributions made by so many people? How to truly acknowledge the importance of others to this project? Like all books, this book reflects not only our own thoughts, work, and experience, but also that of countless other people — colleagues and teachers, past and present, research assistants, graduate and undergraduate students, and inspiring scholars, novelists, and authors who, although they may not agree with us, were instrumental in stimulating our reflection. Authors do not live or write in a vacuum. Their writings and ours are permeated with echoes, grace notes, images, and shadows from a lifetime of encounters with significant others. We wish we could name them all, but that would require a book in itself.

Crucial to this project are two very special and talented people who played the most critical role of all. Without the extensive research assistance, challenging feedback, and exceptional editorial skills of Vanessa Nicolai and Faith Butler, this book would not have been possible. There is no way to adequately acknowledge the value and extent of their contribution.

The research on which this book is based was funded by the Social Sciences and Humanities Research Council of Canada, and by Concordia and McGill Universities (internal research grants). We gratefully acknowledge their assistance.

There are a number of other people whose direct contribution to this book we would like to acknowledge with thanks: Jacqueline Reid-Walsh for significant work on Barbie and Nancy Drew, Ann Smith and Michel Boyer for their helpful editorial advice, Marie Gemma, Nancy Mackenzie, and Larry Prochner, for some wonderful data. In addition, the technical assistance of Kathy McElroy from McGill and the help provided by the staff at the Museum of Radio and Television in New York were much appreciated.

We acknowledge with pleasure the contribution of our doctoral students, and we would also like to thank the graduate students who participated in the winter 1994 seminar at McGill on 'Discourse in teacher education'. We were able to explore many of the ideas for this book with them. Equally important is the contribution of our undergraduate students at Concordia and McGill, many of whom have shared with us their drawings and reflections on teachers. The warmth and generosity of students and faculty at Arctic College, North West Territories, Canada, Beit Berl College, Israel, David Livingstone Teachers'

Acknowledgments

College, Zambia, and the Faculty of Education, University of Zimbabwe, will never be forgotten. We were also fortunate in being able to share and fine-tune our ideas with members of PACT (Professional Actions and Cultures of Teaching).

A special thank you to Claude Bouchard, a Montreal artist and art educator, who facilitated the collection of children's drawings and generously shared her expertise on children's art with us. Leah Sherman from the Faculty of Fine Arts at Concordia was also very helpful in clarifying important aspects of children's drawings. In addition, we would like to thank Catherine Lawton for her expert help in collecting and organizing the data in the early stages of this project. We gratefully acknowledge the 600 (or more) school children and their teachers who contributed to our project. Their colourful drawings and helpful comments proved invaluable, as did the inspirational painting by Deirdre Mackay that is on the cover.

There are many colleagues and friends whose support and friendship has meant a great deal: Lavy, Ilana, and Henry Abramovitch, Stephen Carey, Louise Edwards, Judith Kinghorn, Margaret McNay, Margaret Nicolai, Claudette Tardif, and Rhona Small.

We are especially grateful to Ardra Cole, David Dillon, Ivor Goodson, Henry Giroux, Amadeo Giorgi, Andy Hargreaves, Gary Knowles, Max van Manen, and Marvin Wideen for their encouragement and helpful feedback and advice. We would like to thank Jane Miller for so graciously agreeing to write an introduction, and we are also very thankful for the patience and expertise of Malcolm Clarkson and Jackie Day of Falmer Press.

Finally, this book would not have been possible without the loving support and remarkable patience of our families. Many thanks to the Boyer, Mitchell, Krenz, Reider, Smith, and Weber families.

Foreword

Teachers are figures of such impossible familiarity that they are apt to vanish beneath the general and the particular disparagements such taken-for-granted phenomena may attract to themselves. For many of us who teach, and who have spent much of our lives in schools and amongst teachers, it is their flesh and blood and sweat that haunt us, their actual, historical existence and the work they do with children in classrooms. Yet that reality is shaped and shadowed by all those others: by the transformations performed on teachers by memory and myth, by public obloquy and popular culture and by all the fantasies and fictions which have constructed childhoods for us, and which have then allowed us to scrutinize and revisit the contradictions that those fictions embody. And what is always a surprise at this end of the twentieth century is how many of those fictions turn out to be ones we've not just found or made for ourselves, but ones which we share, through film and television and other media, with most of the human race, however vast all the other differences between us may be.

I was always a little hurt, I think, as a young teacher, when in drama lessons with my eleven-year-olds, their warm-up actings-out — of policemen and bicycles and puppets and, yes, of teachers — produced (and without a single exception) a finger-wagging harridan of quite exceptional vindictiveness. Where, I wondered, had they come upon the model for such a teacher? Surely, it couldn't be . . . ?

Sandra Weber and Claudia Mitchell from Canada, which will always be the land of *Ann of Green Gables* and of *Avonlea* to me, have written a marvellously illuminating book which undertakes, amongst other things, to reassure me. Much more than that, it unpicks and displays the anomalous links between all our classroom realities and the curious and constant and invariably ambiguous recurrence of teachers within a whole range of popular cultural forms. The book's focus is, as the authors put it, on 'the ways that certain images persist over time, and the significance of the continuity of these popular culture images to our understanding of the space that teachers occupy in the real and imagined lives of children and their teachers.'

Wittily and persuasively they present us with a Barbie doll you can dress as a music teacher with appropriate accessories, a teacher of geography surrounded by apples or even a student teacher assigned to give a practice lesson on art history. How are we to read the infinite substitutions of herself that

Barbie is capable of, and what do they tell us about the women she so casually stands in for? What happens to the kindergarten teacher when she is suddenly displaced by an Arnold Schwarzenegger, who is, of course, magically enabled to manage a class of small children without training or preparation? There is the protean teacher of popular children's fiction, at once a creature of romance and an all-powerful witch. And there is the painful exposure of all our assumptions about gender when we return to those legendary teachers of our youth, who may turn out to be men and women somewhat less benign than we remember them.

History provides some explanations for the contradictory memories and valuings of teachers in North American and British culture. What history has difficulty with is the living of doubleness and opposition by teachers themselves and by the children they teach. As adults we are constantly called upon to revisit and remake our childhoods in the light of new recognitions of what may be simultaneously idiosyncratic and communal in what we remember and know. A Cultural Studies approach looks at the dynamic interaction between our readings of cultural forms and the scope of individual and social imagination in relation to them. Here, representations of teachers, drawn by children and by young women and men who are in training to be elementary teachers, provide the data for such an analysis. 'We end up,' as the authors put it,

> not with a sharp composite image of teacher, but with a kaleidoscopic collage of fuchsia shirts, hairnets and buns, bulging biceps, long shapeless dresses, sparkling brown eyes, magic wands, tender smiles. And always, the eternal chalkdust, pointers, apples, and numbers.

It is not often that books are written about education which entertain while they teach. I think of my poor great-aunt Clara, who, already teaching in the early 1880s and required to take examinations for her degree and for her teaching certificate, reports to her diary a most uncharacteristic 'fit of hysterical crying'. Later, she glosses this outburst: 'the literature of educational theorists was responsible for this inspissated gloom'. We all know what she means. There will be no fear of that with this serious and captivating study of the signs and portents conveyed by all those artefacts which connect children with teachers and teachers with their own formation.

Jane Miller
University of London Institute of Education, 1995

1 The Cumulative Cultural Text of Teacher

'I bet she wears orthopedic shoes and glasses an inch thick' Jessica Wakefield told her twin sister, Elizabeth. 'You're exaggerating, Jess', Elizabeth replied calmly, reaching into her locker for her books. 'She'll probably be really nice'. 'Nice? Not a chance', Jessica scoffed. 'The Hairnet wouldn't pick a nice student-teacher. She probably picked someone who gives more homework than she does . . .'

Behind the teacher's desk sat Mrs. Arnette ('the Hairnet'). She looked as reserved as usual, her hair in a neat bun. But walking over to her was a tall, slender girl who looked like a model. The girl leaned over Mrs. Arnette's shoulder and began talking as she smoothed back a strand of curly blond hair. She was wearing a fuchsia zip-front shirt, tight black leggings, and funky black shoes.

'Gee, look at those orthopedic shoes, Jessica', Elizabeth whispered to her twin, barely holding back a smile. 'Come on, Lizzie, she can't be the student teacher. No teacher would wear clothes as great as those!'. (Suzanne, 1992, pp. 1–3)

Why wouldn't a teacher wear a fuchsia zip-front shirt and funky black shoes? Why couldn't she have long, curly blond hair or look like a model? These opening paragraphs are taken from the novel *Barnyard Battle*, one of dozens of books conceived by author Francine Pascal as part of her popular *Sweet Valley High* series. The series has been translated into several languages and is read by millions of young adolescent girls around the world. Using a widely-shared code of cultural markers such as gender (female), appearance (ugly: orthopaedic shoes, inch-thick glasses, hair tied back in a neat bun), and behaviour (unfriendly), the short excerpt from the book introduces the very familiar image of teacher-as-anti-hero in the person of the Hairnet, an authoritarian, joyless woman who embodies much of what many people conjure up when they hear the word 'teacher'. Using the literary device of contrast, the excerpt also presents a counter-image in the form of the stylish substitute teacher, a 'with-it' heroine who is a complete opposite to the Hairnet on almost every count. Where do these images come from, and what is their impact on their audiences and on the profession they depict?

Like the too-good-to-be-true student teacher described above, the woman on the front cover of this book couldn't possibly be a teacher, could she? We might be willing to overlook her loose, blond hair, but can we pardon her red silk negligee and her sensual, revealing pose? Her somewhat erotic pose seems to occur naturally, self-sufficiently in private, asleep alone with her books and dreams, and her apple. And what about the apple? What are we to make of that multilayered signifier that has been used to evoke the temptation of Eve — woman as weak-willed, woman as temptress or seductress, woman as betrayer. What does this fruit that has signified a fall from grace have to do with school? What did Eve find so tempting about the apple in the first place? The power of knowledge? The forbidden? Quenching the thirst of curiosity? Has the knowledge of right and wrong got something to do with teacher? Do male teachers receive apples? Do apples signify a recognition of the teacher as knower, and as moral guide? Are they food for the mind as well as the body? Or is the apple a bit of revenge or bribe — a teasing reminder to teachers that they must be asexual, lest they give in to their weak-willed natures? Does the apple convey the student's plea to the teacher: 'Tempt me too, share your knowledge!'. The multiplicity of possible readings contributes to the power and longevity of certain symbols and images.

The picture and title on the cover of this book hint at the possibility of rupturing everyday preconceptions of teachers, confronting them with images of actual people who make teaching their profession. But teachers not only play a prominent role as real people in the everyday lives of children at school, they are also embedded in many of the books, games, dramatic play, movies, and television shows that form part of children's activities before and after school. Even before children begin school, they have already been exposed to a myriad of images of teachers, classrooms and schools which have made strong and lasting impressions on them.

Caught in their all too real existence somewhere in the vast in-between of the Hairnet and fuchsia zippered shirts, teachers are often aware of the preconceptions and images others hold of them. They may even be aware that their practice is influenced by children's expectations of what teachers are 'supposed' to look like and do. Commonplace remarks we have heard include: 'I don't want to be an authority figure but the children make me'; or 'I don't want to teach in this way, but this is what the children expect me to do'. As Britzman (1986) observes:

> Students construct images of the teacher's world . . . On the classroom level, it is a rare teacher who lends students insight into her/his own teaching struggles. Consequently, what students tend to observe is a pattern that results from the hidden influences of teacher preparation, school policy, curricular mandates, and state law . . . Years of classroom experience allow students to have very specific expectations of how teachers should act in the classroom . . . In this sense, students do coach their teachers in ways which reinforce school structure and, as such, constitute an immediate source of teacher socialization. (p. 445)

A scene from a television episode of the American situation comedy *Boy Meets World* further illustrates the dynamics of student-teacher relationships and expectations in the elementary classroom:

> While waiting for their teacher to enter the classroom, 11-year-old Cory Matthews declares to his friends that being a sixth-grade social studies teacher must be easy work — 'after all, it's the same stuff every year'. He brags to his friends that he can predict exactly what their teacher, Mr. Feeney, will do when he comes into the classroom: He'll stop off at the water fountain, take a drink, wipe his moustache and then say, 'Mr. Matthews, how is the homework?' Indeed, a few seconds later, this is exactly what Mr. Feeney does. What we also find out however, is that following 'Mr. Matthews, how is the homework?', Cory responds 'all done sir, only . . .'. 'I know', interrupts Mr. Feeney, 'only your little sister ate it. So predictable!'. (Fieldnotes)

We see such a scene as a meta-statement about presentation and representation of teaching: students bring certain expectations with them to school, and teachers act on preconceptions of student expectations. Teachers know, for example, that they are reputed to have 'eyes in the back of their heads' and often trade on this knowledge, using the myth to keep children 'on their toes'. This type of myth emanates from a traditional conception of teachers as superhuman role models who exist in a separate dimension from the everyday world. According to this model, teachers live in the classroom, and never have to do ordinary things like go to the bathroom, or buy groceries, or show emotion. They certainly never lie languorously on the floor wrapped in silk. Although pedagogy has supposedly changed over the years, and teachers are more often considered to be 'real people', there are still many things that do not seem 'teacherly'.

The dialogue from *Barnyard Battle* quoted at the beginning of this chapter not only revealed a caricatured and somewhat archaic image of teacher-as-anti-hero, but also a stereotypical student reaction to such a person: Jessica and Elizabeth speak in a mocking, deprecatory tone, and show a strong resentment toward the Hairnet who gives a lot of homework and would never pick a 'nice' student teacher. In the popular culture of childhood, there are many songs and chants displaying varying degrees of hostility towards teachers, that are gleefully passed on from one generation of students to the next:

> 12 and 12 are 24
> Kick the teacher out the door
> If she tries to come back in
> throw her in the garbage bin
> If she tells you 'don't do that'
> hit her with a baseball bat

Row, row, row your boat
Gently down the stream
Throw your teacher overboard
And listen to him scream.

Mine eyes have seen the glory of the burning of the school.
We have tortured all the teachers, we have broken every rule.
We are marching to the office now to kill the principal
On (brand X) lager beer.

These chants cheerfully parody the verses and hymns of well-meaning educators, replacing the authoritarian power of the boring, mean-spirited teacher with vengeful fantasies of student rebellion, tyranny, and even murder. Indeed, as Opie (1993) documents, and as Grugeon (1993) observes, 'the playground might be seen as a site of a subversive counter culture to the official school culture . . . Teachers are in the front line of attack' (p. 15).

We could, and often do, dismiss such rhymes as innocuous ways for children to blow off steam and delight in the illicit pleasure of being naughty, bonding together to assert themselves against adult culture. But even as we dismiss them, we can't help asking what images and conceptions of teachers and schooling make these rhymes possible, and give them such vitality and enduring popularity? We can't help noticing that representations of teachers in popular culture contain paradoxical elements of pleasure, desire, play, violence, and sex, despite common stereotypes of teachers as drab, asocial and asexual creatures whose sole mission is to make children learn, whether they want to or not.

When they were children themselves, many of today's teachers probably took as much delight as today's children do in making fun of their teachers through the very same rhymes. Similarly, like children all over, many teachers played school when they were children or watched movies and television shows about teachers. Now, years later, as adults, they can continue to watch those same shows as reruns, while their students may be rushing home after school to watch them too. Turn on a television, and you could be watching new programs about teachers, or re-runs of ones that your son's or daughter's own teacher watched as a child. Open up the comic section of a newspaper in 1995 and see the same Miss Grundy in the *Archie* comic strip familiar to several generations of adults, including teachers. Memories of such fictional teachers are often more vivid than real life experiences. In a *Hi and Lois* comic strip, for example, where Hi and Lois are attending an open house at their son Ditto's school, we see the following dialogue:

Lois: How could you forget Ditto's teacher's *name*?
Hi: I don't know . . . I guess as I get older my memory gets more selective.
Lois: What *do* you remember?

Hi: The name of the teacher on *Leave it to Beaver* (a television show from the 1950s) was Miss Landers. (*The Gazette*, Montreal, June 14, 1994)

Ironically, many children who claim to hate school watch cartoons featuring teachers before they go to school, or stay up late at night to watch programs set in a school environment (for example, *Beverly Hills 90210*). Several popular television programs in Britain feature school settings and are scheduled at exactly the time that children arrive home from school. As long as it's not 'real' school, many children, especially girls, will voluntarily devote an extraordinary amount of time to consuming images of teaching. Auchmuty (1992) has done a study on the continuing popularity of certain books, such as the school stories by Enid Blyton and Elsie Oxenham. Unlike mandatory school texts, which are often resented and wilfully ignored, these books are read under the covers, after 'lights out', for personal pleasure.

From schoolyard rhymes to 'let's play school', there is a wealth of varied and sometimes contradictory images of teachers that continues to be passed on from one generation to the next. These images have remained largely unexamined and their significance unnoticed. By exposing and probing the dialectical relationship between schooling and the popular culture of everyday life, we explore the socially constructed knowledge of teachers and teaching that is not confined to school buildings, but spills out into television studios, movie theatres, homes, and playgrounds, infiltrating all arenas of human activity. Our work stems from the obvious but underexamined fact that all of today's teachers were once children and some of today's children will be tomorrow's teachers. Locating our work within a framework that draws on cultural studies, critical theory, and literary criticism, we explore the ways in which the images of teachers enculturated in childhood affect the work and professional self-identity of teachers.

Childhood, Teachers and Stereotypes

There is a growing recognition that becoming a teacher begins long before people ever enter a Faculty of Education (for example, Britzman, 1986; Bullough, Knowles and Crow, 1991; Cole and Knowles, 1994; Connelly and Clandinin, 1990; Day, 1990; Goodson and Walker, 1991; Hargreaves and Fullan, 1992; Raymond, Butt and Townsend, 1992; Zeichner and Tabachnick, 1981). However, the images of schooling in everyday life outside of school are often neglected, and treated as if they were on the other side of the line that divides school from 'non-school'. Although some scholars acknowledge the value of studying popular movies in relation to teaching and teacher education (for example, Brunner, 1991; Crume, 1988; Giroux, 1993b; Giroux and Simon, 1989a; Robertson, 1994), almost nothing has been written about the significance of the culture of childhood to teacher identity and teacher education.

The significance of childhood itself is often given lip service, but is not pursued seriously by teacher educators and other scholars. The transcription and critical examination of childhood memories, for example, has only recently become an important part of teacher education. As van Manen (1990) asks:

> Is it not odd that educational researchers often seem to need to overlook the children's interests . . . in order to pursue their research careers which are supposed to be in the interests of children? (p. 90)

Writing about the play and popular culture of childhood within a cultural studies framework, Ellen Seiter (1993) takes up Thorstein Veblen's theory of 'doubtful legitimacy' to account for the exclusion of childhood culture from serious analysis. Seiter asserts that the culture of groups considered to be socially inferior has been characterized as trivial and irrational throughout history. Children are seldom ranked highly in terms of social status and respect. Their culture is not often considered of great import to serious adult scholarship.

The culture of childhood is neither fixed nor static. It does however have a rootedness and history that ensure its survival, and is interwoven with images, especially the pervasive, mass-produced images of popular culture. Walter Benjamin has noted society's tendency to disparage elements from previous periods which seem so outmoded as to be meaningless and alien, and which threaten to disappear irretrievably (in Gilman, 1985, p. 239). Yet, as he goes on to say, images of the past do not really disappear in the sense of ceasing to exist. They may be altered or assimilated, and might eventually become invisible, but just as individual words carry multiple meanings and usages, so images of the present are layered with images of the past, although we may not be aware that this is so. Today's juvenile fiction contains images, structures, and value systems that are at least partially shaped by their earlier counterparts: The ghosts of Mr. Chips, Mr. Gradgrind, and Ichabod Crane silently slip in and out of subsequent texts.

One obvious reason for this continuity is that the adult writers of contemporary children's fiction were once themselves child readers of fiction written for them by a previous generation. Thus, each generation of children's authors, and film and television producers are in some ways responding to what they themselves experienced as young consumers of popular culture. This intergenerational sharing forms a kind of sediment; an underlying repository of past meanings that rubs off on current imagery and understandings, creating a multilayered cumulative effect.

Mitchell and Reid-Walsh (1994; in press) draw our attention to the significance of this cumulative effect by coining the term 'cumulative cultural text' to describe the intergenerational and intertextual nature of popular children's fiction series. We extend their work to include more explicitly other series such as television, movies, records, and toys, and we slightly reformulate the cumulative features they identify as being characteristic of children's fiction series. The potential of series as cumulative cultural texts can be seen as follows:

(i) *Series as episodic.* A series is comprised of a sequence of episodes, individual books or shows or albums or items, that cumulatively form a single text. *Archie* comics, *Beatles* albums collections, the *Power Ranger* television series, and *Star Wars* films are but a few examples. Both implicitly and explicitly, individual episodes contextualize, influence, build on, and refer to each other, collaboratively constituting the cumulative text (series).

(ii) *Series as 'rite of passage' within a social and historical network.* The *Nancy Drew* and *Hardy Boys* book series, for example, have been read by three-and-a-half generations of readers, and new episodes continue to be produced. For many 9–12-year-old readers they are a type of 'rite of passage'. Parents often acknowledge and participate in this rite, by passing on their own memories and copies of earlier versions of the series to their children, contributing to a cross-generational cumulative text. Long-running television shows such as *Star Trek* or *Coronation Street*, toys like Barbie dolls and accessories, and the concerts and albums of groups like the *Rolling Stones* offer similar opportunities for rites of passage and intergenerational rituals.

(iii) *Series as generative and multi-dimensional.* The cultural text of a series also includes the many related 'spin-off' products such as games, diaries, dolls, books, movies, action figures, lunch kits, computer software and television series that may be generated by the popularity of the original series. Miss Stacey, for example, was a teacher in the book series *Anne of Green Gables* long before she became a character in a related television series, as well as in a stage musical. *My Little Pony* was sold as a toy before a tie-in television cartoon series was developed. The original eleven-and-a-half-inch Barbie doll was soon accompanied by a series of 'spin-off' texts, including clothing, lifestyle paraphernalia, comic books, collector cards, exercise videos, and the like.

(iv) *Series as intertextual.* Some of the images and characters from popular series are so pervasive or ubiquitous that they turn up in other unrelated series and contexts as part of the language of popular culture. Thus, for example, the intertextual nature of the *Archie* comic book series is revealed when a teacher in an unrelated book or movie is described as a 'Miss Grundy' type. In everyday discourse, a woman may be referred to as a 'Barbie-type'. Critics of the *Nancy Drew Files* series argue that Nancy has become 'Barbie-fied'. The images from one series or episode seep into another, becoming incorporated into an even larger cumulative cultural text.

We extend the notion of cumulative cultural text even further to include teacher and teaching as cultural texts. The multitude of images that occur and recur throughout the various 'texts' of teaching accompany us throughout our lives. Contemporary popular culture subsumes not only the culture of today's children and adults, but also a vast text of culture from the past which blends seamlessly into our familiar, unquestioned everyday knowledge. *Archie* comics, *Welcome Back Kotter*, and Barbie dolls connect generations of teachers (former children) and children (as students and future teachers), marking experience with codes and signposts that are casually shared, passed down, and assimilated in a subconscious, taken-for-granted manner. It is the longevity and resilience of certain images of teaching in this cumulative cultural text called 'teacher' that interest us, particularly because of the significance of childhood culture to becoming a teacher.

The importance of studying stereotypes and cliches in cultural texts is acknowledged by Sander Gilman (1985) who asserts that:

> Texts are an ideal source for a study of the fluidity of stereotypical concepts . . . 'text' must be understood in the broadest sense of that term. All structured systems of representation, no matter what the medium, can be construed as 'texts' for the study of stereotypes. (p. 26)

The significance of stereotypes and cliches in the cultural text of teaching emanates from the work of scholars such as Dana Polan (1993) who focus on ways in which they contribute to the construction of the classroom:

> For many students, the teacher is not a conduit to knowledge that exists elsewhere: the teacher is an image, a cliche in the sense both of stereotype but also photographic imprinting that freezes knowledge in the seeming evidence of a look, where the image predetermines what the person means to us. . . . The medium is the message, and the image of the professor often matters more than the ideas of the lesson. (Polan, 1993, p. 32)

Our interest is not specifically in 'debunking' the myths, stereotypes, and cliches of schooling contained within these texts, for as McRobbie (1992) observes:

> There is no going back . . . For populations transfixed on images which are themselves a reality, there is no return to a mode of representation which politicizes in a kind of straightforward 'worthwhile' way. Dallas is destined to sit alongside images of black revolt. And it is no longer possible, living within postmodernism, to talk about unambiguously negative or positive images. (p. 115)

Our intent is to interrogate the collage of contradictory images, cliches, and stereotypes of teaching in order to probe the ways in which they infiltrate curriculum and the professional identity of teachers. How might we look at texts within this collage as episodes within a larger text? In what ways do such texts work intertextually and intergenerationally? How do the texts of teaching in the play and popular culture of childhood contribute to a cumulative cultural text of teaching? In examining the texts and counter-texts of schooling and popular culture, we will frame unexpected dialogues between the 'inside' and 'outside' of classroom culture, between 'illicit' and 'prescribed' culture, and between teachers as former consumers of teacher images and students as present consumers of teacher images.

Collective Biography

As Britzman (1986) notes, teachers bring to teaching not only their personal biographies, but also:

> their implicit institutional biographies — the cumulative experience of school lives — which, in turn, inform their knowledge of the student's world, of school structure, and of curriculum. All this contributes to well-worn and commonsensical images of the teacher's work and serves as the frame of reference for prospective teachers' self-images. But the dominant model of teacher education as vocational training does not address the hidden significance of biography in the making of a teacher, particularly as it is lived during student teaching . . . I argue that the underlying values which coalesce in one's institutional biography, if unexamined, propel the cultural reproduction of authoritarian teaching practices and naturalize the contexts which generate such a cycle. (p. 443)

Writing in different veins about the culture of teaching, several authors (e.g. Cole and Knowles, 1994; Goodson and Walker, 1991; Hargreaves and Fullan, 1992; Weber, 1993) remind us that our stories are not only our own personal accounts; we live embedded in biographies that are simultaneously personal, cultural, institutional, and historical. Our identities as teachers stem from both individual and collective life history.

In an unorthodox fashion, this book could be labelled biographical. It is based on a cultural studies reading of the textual representations or images that form a collective biography of teachers, revealing the contributions of social, fictional, fantasy, and private worlds to the construction of the cumulative cultural text called teacher. The text of this book includes images of teachers in movies, books, toys, television, children's play, and in people's memories, writing, and drawings. By interrogating and juxtaposing images from popular culture with the words and life experience of both children and teachers, we write a sort of collective autobiography, replete with stereotypes of heroes and superheroes, romantic figures, villains, monsters, and witches.

This collective autobiography embraces several forbidden themes, including gender, romance, and sexuality. For example, although television and movies are populated with many heroic male teachers, there are almost no female counterparts. Yet since the nineteenth century, particularly in North America, Britain, Europe, and Australia, early childhood and elementary school teaching has largely been the domain of women. Whether they have been seeking higher salaries, greater status and power, and a more masculine image, or whether they were attracted to the more 'serious' curriculum of high school, men in most countries have largely abandoned elementary schooling to women.

As we argue throughout this book, while teachers figure in the play and popular culture of both boys and girls, they occupy a particularized, gendered space in the play and popular culture of girls. Writing about images of elementary teachers thus necessarily means writing about women and women's culture. But men, too, are integral to a discussion of the culture of elementary school teaching, especially by virtue of 'the presence of their absence' from the classroom, and their dominance of the principal's office. We discuss the impact of the feminization of early childhood and elementary school teaching on both sexes, and the implications for teacher education. In short, we bring to this book a juxtapositioning of themes and an acknowledgment of cultures that have traditionally been excluded from the discourse of teacher education: childhood and popular culture; play and schooling; sex, pleasure and pedagogy; the illicitness of popular culture and the prescribed structures of schooling; the simultaneously conservative and revolutionary forces in mass culture and schooling.

About Cultural Studies

Using the image of performance as a metaphor for human behaviour in everyday social interaction, Goffman (1959) writes:

> when an individual plays a part (s)he implicitly requests her/his observers to take seriously the impression that is fostered before them. They are asked to believe that the character they see actually possesses the attributes (s)he appears to possess, that the tasks (s)he performs will have the consequences that are implicitly claimed for it, and that, in general, matters are what they appear to be. (p. 17)

A cultural studies orientation to the texts of teaching acknowledges the classroom as a cultural site within which performances take place. Our exploration of performance texts of teaching both inside and outside of the classroom rests on what Richard Johnson describes as a type of double articulation of culture, 'where culture is simultaneously the ground on which analysis proceeds, the object of study, and the site of political critique and intervention' (cited in Grossberg, Nelson, and Treichler, 1992, p. 5). Fiske (1987b) asserts that 'the term "culture" used in the phrase "cultural studies" is neither aesthetic nor humanistic in emphasis, but political' (p. 254).

The study of popular culture is located within questions of ideology. For example, in what ways do mass-produced texts contribute to a particular construction of gender, consumerism, schooling, or authority, to name but a few ideological 'hot spots'? Cultural studies addresses both the ideologies of 'the ruling class' as well as the ideologies of resistance. The texts of popular culture are located in daily life, excluded from the canonized texts of the academy, art, and literature. Because they are situated in the everyday, the social context in which popular texts are read and critically received may be even more important than the texts themselves which are often assumed to be shallow, formulaic and unidimensional. How does the line dividing canonized from non-canonized texts come to be? Who draws it and why? How is it maintained? What is the nature of the non-canonized texts on the 'wrong' side of the line? The accessibility of popular texts, both in terms of their availability and comprehensibility makes them ideally suited to investigation.

A few scholars have focused on the representation of teachers and pedagogy in popular culture. Movies seem to have attracted the most attention. For example, a survey done in 1959 of teachers in Hollywood films identified eighty-one films which feature teachers either as main characters or as important supporting characters (Gerbner, 1963). More recent studies on films about teachers include Crume's (1988) study of twenty-eight films depicting high school teachers (for example, *The Breakfast Club*), and Brunner's (1991) analysis of ten films on teachers using a critical theory lens. Giroux (1993b), through his critique of the powerful movies *Dead Poets Society* and *Stand and Deliver*, has demonstrated the value of a critical stance to educators. Extending their analysis of images of teachers in twentieth century America beyond movies to other forms of popular culture, Joseph and Burnaford (1994b) survey television programs and other image sources, including some from the popular culture of childhood.

The play and popular culture of childhood provide a rich corpus of teaching texts that permeate, infiltrate, rupture and accumulate in the history of teaching. Why don't we know more about the ways in which we as teachers occupy the consciousness of children? Why don't we know more about the ways in which the popularity of schooling outside school contributes to classroom dialogues between teachers and students? And who should be asking these questions, if not the people who work in teacher education?

Our analytical framework draws on the work of John Fiske (1987a) who argues that a 'cultural reading' should address three levels of textuality: *primary texts* (books, movies, television, etc.); *secondary or cultural production texts* (for example, fan magazines, publicity, criticism), and *tertiary or reader texts* (the writing, reactions and speech of readers or viewers themselves, for example, discussions about television programs, letters to the editor, adoption of styles of dress, speech, or even of thinking). Of equal importance to Fiske is the contextual relationships among these three levels which constitute their intertextuality. These levels 'leak into each other', demanding, in a sense, to be read together. Cultural studies aims to understand and encourage this cultural democracy at work.

As Foff (1956) points out, teachers and educators need to know how others see them through the media for their own professional identity. Novels (especially bestsellers) and motion pictures are likely to reach a far greater audience than scholarly studies. These fictional media have the potential to reveal the inner life of the teacher with a depth and emotion that are usually missing from quantitative sociological studies. Through the lives of their fictional counterparts, teachers can better understand themselves and others, and the nature of their practice.

Collecting and Recollecting Images/Texts of Schooling

We realized just how pervasive schooling is outside of school when we began telling people about our research project. Students, friends, colleagues, family members, and even our children's friends inundated us with comic strips, video clips of Saturday morning cartoons and popular shows for children, school songs, rock songs, and children's books — all of these items featuring teachers. People began remembering and telling us about television shows from their own childhood experiences. Some of these programs, like *Our Miss Brooks* and *Room 222*, were organized around schools; others, like *Leave It To Beaver*, contained episodes about teaching simply because they were shows about the lives of children, and most children sooner or later go to school. Younger informants, including our own children, would call out 'there's a teacher on T.V.' and we would rush in to view the latest episode of *My Little Pony, Boy Meets World*, or *Road to Avonlea, The Magic Bus*.

More systematically, we consulted the archives of the Museum of Radio and Television in New York, which has an impressive video collection of episodes of television shows from the late 1940s to the present. We spent three fascinating days there watching reruns of *Our Miss Brooks, Leave it to Beaver, Welcome Back Kotter*, and *Mr. Peepers*. We even found teachers in an episode of *The Twilight Zone*, that we immediately recognized as the precursor to the popular *Back to the Future* movies.

As we began analyzing our large collection of teaching images, we realized that in a sense we were gazing at representations of ourselves and the teachers with whom we work in our undergraduate and graduate university classes. Yet, we feel very different and distant from most of those images. If those are teachers, we certainly don't look like them, or at least don't want to admit to looking like them. But certain doubts begin to creep into our minds. Do we, as teachers, unconsciously project images like those we disown? How do our student teachers see us? What images lurk in the back of their minds and colour their perceptions of us as people and as professionals? As professors, how exactly are we supposed to look, feel, and act?

One of the few images we found of a Professor of Education is from a scene of an old film *The Blackboard Jungle*, where Mr. Dadier, a beginning high school teacher, returns to university to ask his professor what he should do about the juvenile delinquents he feels unprepared to teach. His professor fits the stereotypical image of an elderly, absent-minded, rather ineffectual man who is out of touch, shut up in an ivory tower. After admitting to the possibility that the university does not prepare teachers for the realities of the urban classroom, the best advice Mr. Dadier's mentor can offer is the half-hearted assurance, 'you'll find a way'. As Polan (1993) argues, university professors, like teachers, enter a classroom that is already laden with representation, both in their own heads as well as in the heads of their students:

> From the cliches that precede the professor into the classroom to the larger codes of mass communication, there is no site of knowledge production unshaped by conventions, disembodied from public image and representation. The need for the intellectual, then, is not to imagine that there is some pristine space of pure pedagogy nor to act as if knowledge is so important in and of itself that it forces such a space into being. The need, rather, is for intellectuals to begin to reflect upon their own embodiment, to understand how knowledge, their own knowledge, is fully situated, and how to build from the givens of their situation a responsible and attentive pedagogy. (p. 47)

This sudden self-consciousness made us even more sensitive to other people's preoccupations with expectations, images, and appearances and prompted us to include our own experiences as fair game for analysis. We soon discovered that we are not alone in addressing schooling in folk and popular culture. A small but growing number of scholars in teacher education have become interested in images of schooling beyond the classroom. Note-worthy works in the literature include Farber, Provenzo and Holm's (1994) *Schooling in the Light of Popular Culture*, Joseph and Burnaford's (1994b) *Images of Schoolteachers in 20th Century America*, articles such as Giroux's (1993b) 'Reclaiming the social: Pedagogy, resistance, and politics in celluloid culture', Brunner's (1991) 'Stories of schooling in film and television', Crume's (1988) dissertation 'Images of teachers in novels and films for the adolescent, 1980–1987', and Robertson's (1994) dissertation, 'Cinema and the politics of desire in teacher education'. This literature addresses, for the most part, mainstream popular culture, particularly Hollywood films, whereas we focus more specifically on the popular culture of childhood. However, in keeping with Fiske's notion that texts leak into each other, our work on the popular culture of childhood embraces and speaks to the work of colleagues such as those cited above.

It is also important to acknowledge that scholars outside education have been interested in images of teachers and schooling in children's texts for several decades, especially images emanating from the genre of the 'British school story'. Much of their work falls into the literary tradition, for example, Quigly's (1982) *The Heirs of Tom Brown's School Days*, Auchmuty's (1992) *The World of Girls*, Gathorne-Hardy's (1977) *The Public School Phenomenon*, Cadogan and Craig's (1986) *You're a Brick, Angela: The Girls' Story 1939–1985*, Reynolds' (1990) *Girls' Only? Gender and Popular Children's Fiction in Britain, 1880–1910*, and Musgrave's (1985) *From Brown to Bunter: The Life and Death of the School Story*. Equally important are collections such as Craig's (1994) *Oxford Book of Schooldays* and Booth's (1993) *Dr. Knickerbocker and Other Rhymes*, which have been particularly helpful for situating schooling in the history of children's literature.

So pervasive are teachers in popular culture that if you simply ask, as we have, schoolchildren and adults to name teachers they remember, not from school but from popular culture, a cast of fictionalized characters emerges that takes on larger than life proportions. Each generation reveals its own icons. We asked children born in the early eighties to describe teachers from popular culture: 'Have you ever read any books or watched TV shows or movies about teachers or teaching?; Can you name these books, shows, or movies?; What did you think of the teacher in the book, movie or TV show?' Their answers indicated that indeed teachers have a prime-time significance outside the classroom, and that children are exposed to a variety of images of teaching. Commenting on a teacher from the then popular television show *The Wonder Years*, one of the students observed:

> 1.1. She wouldn't follow the school rules, she didn't give them actual grades like pass or fail. I like that. She was a good teacher who got the children to learn. (Karen, 10)

Several students remarked that Anne (from the movie *Anne of Green Gables*), 'was a very good and exciting teacher, a good tutor'. Many teachers from books were also mentioned, including '. . . very mean and bossy' teachers from the *Baby-sitter's Club* series, Anne Shirley ('a very good teacher'), from *Anne of Avonlea*, Stuart, the substitute teacher from *Stuart Little*, who is 'only a teacher for one day but he's good', and the teachers from *Ramona the Pest*, who 'were very different from our teachers in real life'. We asked similar questions to student teachers in our education classes: 'Describe teachers that you remember from books, films and T.V. What do these memories mean to you? How important are they to your teaching?' Many of these students named Mr. Keating (*Dead Poets Society*), Mr. Thackeray (*To Sir With Love*), and Mr. Escalante (*Stand and Deliver*).

As Crume (1988) observes, no single text is necessarily accessed by all people for all time. Gender, class, and even parents' television viewing rules, all mediate the reading and viewing habits of children. Our questions moved away from which texts to analyze to a consideration of the content of the texts, and how cultural conventions are used. It was not enough, we decided, to examine or even interrogate popular culture alone. How could we trace the influence of popular images on people's conceptions and attitudes? How could we get at the images of teacher that children and teachers form in the course of their everyday lives? In other words, how could we access the consumers' point of view, or what Fiske describes as reader texts?

Playing the Texts of Teaching

These questions made us extend rather than limit our investigation. For example, pretend-play and drawing are two ways in which young children make sense of their world. Examining these phenomena in relation to teachers and schooling might thus provide a point of entry to children's views of teachers. Consider, for example, the following description of a child playing school, an episode told to us in an interview by the mother of a 3½-year-old boy:

> Michel is playing school with his Fisher Price 'little people' figurines and playhouse. He has meticulously arranged fourteen little people in one of the bedrooms of the playhouse. All fourteen little people, varying in sex, age, and ethnicity are standing at the back of the room. All face the front. They are positioned in three rows. From his collection, Michel then selects one more little person, and places it at the other end of the room facing the fourteen others. This little person is white and female. She is the teacher; the fourteen others are her students. As Michel's play episode begins, two more 'little people' approach the 'school' and knock on the door. One of the little people represents Michel; the other his father:
>
> | | |
> |---|---|
> | *Teacher*: | Now I'm the teacher. |
> | *Little person*: | Teacher, can we come in? |
> | *Teacher*: | Sure . . . (inaudible. The teacher puts the daddy in jail.) |
> | *Teacher*: | It's time to put the toys away so we can have our snack today. (singing) |
> | *Little person*: | And I'm eating beside my cousin — beside my friend. (Somebody comes to the door) |
> | *Little person*: | Anybody home? . . . Anybody home? . . . Anybody home? |
> | *Teacher*: | No! (annoyed). It's time to go outside the school. |

The students leave the classroom. One little person-student (Michel) is approached by a little person-mother (or someone who appears to represent his mother):

> *Mother*: Oh Michel! Did you have a good time at school?
> *Michel*: Where's Dad?
> *Mother*: He's in jail because he wanted to be in school today.
> *Michel*: Oh! let me go see. (They go to the 'jail')
> *Michel*: Daddy! Hey! Let's go home for lunch . . .

As a preschool teacher and the mother of Michel, Anna, who shared the above scene with us, registers the discrepancy between Michel's representations of teachers and schooling and the presentations of teaching in his everyday preschool experience:

His (preschool) teacher is warm, friendly and speaks to Michel and his classmates with utmost respect. In their classroom there are no desks or rows but rather child-sized round tables, carpeting, lots of toys and interest centres. The program emphasizes play and creative exploration. The children are usually scattered and busy in different areas of the room. When the group does gather, it is usually in circle form on the floor.

In Michel's play, however, the teacher stands at the front of the class. Her students are in rows facing her. Her words, while reflective of pre-school ('Put the toys away'), also set everyone straight as to who is in charge ('Now I'm the teacher'). Not only does the teacher speak in very bossy and domineering tone, she also has the authority to put a father in jail! Although Michel is a boy, he chooses a woman to be the teacher. In a later segment of playing school, Michel insists on 'doing homework', and starts to copy out '1–2–3's'.

We thus see how a $3^1/_2$-year-old child, who has never been to 'big school', already has a strong sense of what school ought to be and how teachers ought to act. He has also worked out something about power relations between males and females in the classroom. By observing children playing school and by inviting adults to recollect and describe their memories of how they played school when they were children, we were afforded a glimpse of how images of teachers and schooling are played out in children's natural sense-making activities. In other words, to refine our interpretation of the images in primary texts such as television programs and books, we investigated the phenomenon of playing school as a reader text that helps access the consumer's point of view.

Drawing the Images of Teaching

A vast collection of drawings of teachers constitutes another reader text that provides insight into how students and teachers read the cultural imagery of teaching. The next two chapters focus on these pictures (over 600) drawn by children, preservice teachers, and experienced teachers. Our collection includes drawings done in Zimbabwe, Zambia, the Canadian Arctic, poor rural areas, and a large multiethnic, multicultural Canadian city. Most of the drawings were done with coloured pencils or crayons on standard blank paper (8½" × 11"). People were invited to 'Draw a teacher (any teacher)', and were then either interviewed ('Tell me about your picture'), or asked to write about their picture, or invited to join a group discussion about who teachers are and what teachers do.

When we initially shared these drawings with colleagues and teachers at conferences (Mitchell and Weber, 1993; Weber and Mitchell, 1993), they often reacted with dismay upon viewing the stereotypical portrayal of teachers in many of the drawings. Not wishing to believe that children are still raised and socialized into these images, they told us that the drawings were artefacts of our study design, and that if we had posed our invitation differently, the children would have provided less stereotypical, portrait-like drawings. Curious, we gathered further samples using the following variations of the directives: 'Please draw your teacher teaching somebody'; 'Please draw your favourite teacher'; 'Please draw your class at work'; 'Please draw an ideal teacher.' These additional samples were also followed up by individual interviews, writing, or group discussion. Although we did get a more frequent and varied inclusion of children in the pictures, the resulting drawings were very similar to the first set insofar as the portrayal of the teacher was concerned.

One major group of drawings we use in this book explores images of teachers held by preservice teachers and by experienced teachers who were enrolled in graduate courses in elementary education at a large Canadian university (1992–93). As part of a reflective log or journal, both groups were simply asked to draw a teacher (any teacher, or themselves as a teacher). They were then asked to write about their drawings, indicating any ideas they had about why they had drawn the pictures the way they had. Some of the graduating student teachers also chose to draw another picture after they had completed their teaching internship.

To compare the drawings, we displayed them on a long wall close to each other in several parallel rows and then repeatedly rearranged them, systematically juxtaposing different sets. Our subsequent analysis thus facilitates a sort of dialogue between children and teachers, between males and females, between different class sets — a contrast and comparison of their views of teachers. The images conveyed by the drawings were further clarified and interrogated in the light of a multiplicity of counter-texts: contextual fieldnotes written during visits to the children's classes, interviews and written comments provided by many of the children, and excerpts from comments made by student teachers and experienced teachers in their journals and teaching logs.

Although, like any written text, drawings are subject to varied interpretations, certain aspects of the database helped to direct our analysis. For instance, classroom visits and interviews with some of the children and teachers about specific drawings, allowed us to identify how children intertwined creative or fanciful aspects with more realistic features that directly reflected their actual schooling experience. For example, Colour plate 1 depicts a female student teacher (of Asian background) as drawn by a twelve-year-old boy in a class she was teaching during her teaching internship. On a separate page she submitted to us with the drawing, this preservice teacher remarks:

> 1.2.   It's funny that he drew me teaching a science experiment. I did a lot of experiments with the class and they really looked forward to them. I guess that is how he will remember me. He apologized for making me brown. He said he did not have the 'right' colour at home for my skin colour. I told him that I thought it was a beautiful drawing of me and that I was a beautiful colour. He seemed to feel happy with this response. It is interesting that he drew me holding a pointer because I never taught using one. Then again, I never wear pink high heels, either. (Dora, student teacher)

Here we see how a child's artistic intentions can simultaneously be a serious effort to represent actual classroom experience (the teacher's skin colour, the science lesson), an intentional use of a culturally powerful marker to signify teacher (the pointer), and a whimsical interpretation of teaching, or of women (pink high heels, the kind you find on Barbie dolls). Most of the drawings we collected had some relationship to real life experiences. For example, drawings done by children sharing the same local context (i.e. teacher and classroom) showed marked resemblances, reflecting the commonality of the children's school experience.

We were surprised to find that the children's and student teachers' drawings were generally quite similar in terms of style and content. Both children and adults used almost identical symbols to depict a teacher, systematically including 'markers' such as blackboards, desks, apples, pointers, maths, and homework. Our collection of drawings did not reveal much cultural variation either: Many of the same markers were found in the drawings done by students from the Canadian Arctic, Zambia, Zimbabwe, inner city schools, posh elite schools, and racially or culturally mixed schools. We began to realize that these markers are part of a Western visual vocabulary that is widely used by several generations to portray a teacher.

Drawings as Texts of Popular Culture

Artistic forms of expression engage our imagination and teach us the commonplaces of our culture. (Joseph and Burnaford, 1994a, p. 8)

Subjectivity and identity are in part constituted on the ground of the popular, and their force and effects do not disappear once students enter school. (Giroux and Simon, 1989b, p. 18)

Drawings are like a mirror of the social images that surround us, especially those portrayed in the media (Wilson and Wilson, 1977). This was recognized decades ago by Mead (1951/1962) who wrote about the power of image in the media, literature, and other forms of popular culture to create our sense of reality of what is possible, normal, usual. The popular becomes part of our very identity, of who we are. This point was illustrated by Adler (1982), who, in a large-scale, international study of children's drawings of fruit trees, found that the majority of children drew apple trees, even in tropical countries where apple trees do not grow. She concluded that although pictures may reflect local experience and personal attitudes, they also mirror existing global social value systems. Since apple trees grow mostly in 'modern' or 'westernized' countries, the almost global appearance of apple trees in children's drawings can be seen as a symbol of the spread and appeal of Westernization and modernization; an appeal that filters down through the media and popular culture even to childhood culture in non-westernized countries. Another crosscultural analysis of children's drawings (Dennis, 1966 and 1970) shows that children would rather depict what they value or prefer in their drawings than what they have actually experienced most. In other words, children (and perhaps adults, as well) will often draw what is culturally desirable and acceptable instead of, or in addition to, simply reflecting their personal environment and the experiences they have had.

Because a picture can communicate simultaneously on many levels, drawings are useful not only as iconic images, but also as layered paintings that hide or combine other social, cultural, and personal images. An analysis of drawings can thus reveal aspects of our personal and social knowledge — how we see the world, how we feel, and what we can imagine — that have largely been ignored.

And so, armed with a vast collection of 'texts' gathered from popular culture, and from the play, writing, interviews, and drawings of children and teachers, we are ready to proceed with a close reading of these texts and the ways in which they infiltrate each other. The images contained within these texts contribute to a cumulative cultural text of teacher.

2   Images, Metaphors, and Stereotypes: The Struggle for Identity

My teacher has a head like a steam pudding baked a bit too much! Her eyes sparkle at you and go right through you, her nose is little and flat like a knob with a pimple on it. When you address her she opens her eyelids and her eyes stare at you. Her eyes say wordlessly: 'Quiet!' sometimes, very rarely, she smiles. But the next second the smile is wiped away, it changes into an embarrassed leer. Her teeth are probably false, because they always hang out. She has a slim, steely body like that of a needle. Small, thin and sharp with an eagle's needle eye. The dresses she wears are very long and frightfully clean. Miniskirts are an abomination to her!

Linda, 12, England (Lepman, 1971, p. 65)

Quick! Think of 'teacher'. What do you see? What does what you see mean? Where does what you see come from? Quick! Think of 'doctor'. What do you see? What does it mean? Where does it come from?

All words have the 'taste' of a profession, a genre, a tendency, a party, a particular work, a particular person, a generation, an age group, the day and hour. Each word tastes of the context in which it has lived its socially charged life: all words and forms are populated by intentions. (Bakhtin, 1986, p. 293)

What is the taste, smell, look, touch, and meaning of 'teacher' these days? What does it matter?

It makes a great deal of difference to our practice . . . if we think of teaching as gardening, coaching, or cooking. It makes a difference if we think of children as clay to mold or as players on a team or as travellers on a journey. (Connelly and Clandinin, 1988, p. 71)

How people think about teaching may be shaped in many ways by the images of teacher in popular culture that they encounter in their daily lives. In this chapter, we explore the power of image and metaphor, especially in relation to teacher identity. While we devote considerable attention in later chapters to the popular culture of childhood, our discussion here will be largely based on the imagery of drawings and of everyday language.

Image and Metaphor in Education

We began this chapter by evoking images in two slightly different ways: We quoted a 12-year-old girl's written description of her 'steam-pudding-head teacher', using her words to paint an image or word-picture representation of a specific teacher. We thus liken the imagery of text with visual images, such as those in art and the physical world of line, shape, and colour. Next, we said: 'Quick! Think of "teacher". What do you see? What does what you see mean? Where does what you see come from?' This line of questioning is central to the use of the word 'image' to refer to an idea, mental representation, or conception that has a visual or physical flavour, an experiential meaning, a context or history, and a metaphorical, generative potential.

Image-making is an essential characteristic of human sense-making (Wilson and Wilson, 1979). Images are constructed and interpreted in attempts to make sense of human experience and to communicate that sense to others. Images in turn become part of human experience, and are thus subject to reconstructions and reinterpretations. While images always maintain some connection to people, places, things, or events, their generative potential in a sense gives them a life of their own, so that we not only create images, but are also shaped by them.

Images exert their generative power largely through their fundamental role in metaphor. Consensus about the nature of metaphor is elusive. As Hawkes (1972, p. 5) points out, 'the notion of metaphor itself is shaped at any given time by linguistic and social pressures, as well as by its own history: it has no pristine form'. Dickmeyer (1989) describes metaphor as:

> a characterization of a phenomenon in familiar terms. To be effective in promoting understanding of the phenomenon in question, the 'familiar terms' must be graphic, visible, and physical in our scale of the world. To characterize teaching as pouring knowledge into the empty vessel of a student is to describe the phenomenon in physical terms at a very 'handy' size. In our imagination, we can see ourselves physically 'doing teaching' in this way. (p. 151)

What implications do images and metaphors hold for teachers and teaching? Several scholars are studying the use of metaphors and images in education (for example, Bullough, Knowles, and Crow, 1991; Elbaz, 1991; Eraut, 1985; Hunt, 1987; Miller and Fredericks, 1988; Munby, 1986; Provenzo, McCloskey, Kottkamp, and Cohn, 1989; Russell and Johnston, 1988). Bullough *et al.* (1991) suggest that, through their metaphorical power, images are both the building blocks of our thinking schemata, and the filters through which we unconsciously assess our pedagogical knowledge. As Elbaz (1991) observes,

> concepts such as 'image' and 'metaphor' speak particularly to the integrated nature of teachers' knowledge in its simultaneously emotional, evaluative and cognitive nature, and also convey the personal meanings which permeate this knowledge. One teacher's sense of her classroom as 'home', another's view of her subject matter sometimes as a 'barrier to hide behind', at other times a 'window on what students are thinking', both allow us to share in the teacher's experience precisely as she sees fit to express it. (p. 13)

Eraut (1985) uses 'image' to refer to the many visual memories or snapshots of children and situations that enter teachers' minds in the course of everyday teaching — what Bandman (1967, p. 112) earlier termed 'picture preferences'. In referring to what they call 'personal practical knowledge', Connelly and Clandinin (1985) say that images become embodied in us, and are expressed in our language and our actions. Johnston (1992) uses 'image' as a way of conceptualizing and understanding the practical knowledge of preservice teachers. She reports that images provide a language for teachers that makes explicit the subconscious assumptions on which practice is based. Calderhead and Robson (1991) note that an image can help to synthesize knowledge about teachers, children, and teaching methods.

Much of the work on metaphor in teacher education centres on the search for appropriate metaphors to conceptualize teaching (for example, gardening versus sculpting). The importance of this search rests on the ability of metaphor to provide both a perspective, or way of looking at things and a process by which new perspectives can emerge (Schön, 1979). Certain scholars propose different schemes for classifying, viewing, or using metaphors. Lawton (1984), for example, proposes three categories of teaching metaphors: *radical* (encouraging change), *conservative* (encouraging stability), and *reactionary* (looking back to a golden age). A more recent classification based on case studies and discussions with teachers is put forward by Fischer & Kiefer (1994, p. 42). They propose two groupings of metaphoric images: those referring to the teaching self (for example, teacher as interpreter, teacher as presence); and those referring to relationships between teacher and students (for example, teacher as advocate, teacher as therapist, teacher as parent, teacher as companion).

Brown (1978) describes three types of metaphors: i. *Analogic metaphors*, which create meaning in terms of comparisons and relationships, suggesting how one thing can be understood in terms of another (for example, schooling as banking or distribution system); ii. *Iconic metaphors*, which provide an image of what things are, rather than creating a new sense of meaning through comparison; and iii. *Root metaphors*, which are sets of usually unrecognized assumptions that organize an individual's views about the world — how it is made up, how it works, and how it may be known. Some people, for example, may subconsciously view events as beyond their control, or, alternatively, as subject to human control.

Referring to Brown's classification, Bowers (1980) provocatively asserts that the very metaphors which are the most fundamental to education are those of which we are the least aware:

> Root metaphors constitute the basic frames of reference or paradigms for making sense of our world, and are the starting point for all theory building. Unlike analogic and iconic metaphors, they usually exist below the level of conscious awareness. (p. 272)

Grant (1992) proposes a similar scheme for looking at metaphors in education based on the notion of 'surface' and 'deep' (or structural) metaphors. Drawing on the work of Schön (1979) and Lakoff & Johnson (1980), he views 'deep' metaphors as those which predominantly shape our understanding and perception of social situations. Grant (1992) refers to these deep metaphors as the 'superorganizer[s] of the concepts teachers use to represent planning, implementing, and managing curriculum activities' (p. 434), and points out that they are often discovered through storytelling, where they present one concept as structured in terms of another (Lakoff and Johnson, 1980).

The categories provided by these and other theorists suggest that there are at least two levels at which a metaphor can operate: one that is more obvious ('surface', or clearly visible), and another that is hidden and more difficult to pinpoint. The meaning of the visible side of the metaphor is largely dependent on the nature of the invisible side, although we are generally unaware of the connection between the two. This duality may account for the strong link between metaphor and ideology noted by Bowers (1980):

> Put succinctly, metaphors always have an ideological basis that gives them their special symbolic power to expand meaning . . . metaphors carry or lay down, in Langer's phrase, 'a deposit of old, abstracted concepts' that reflect the episteme or ideological framework from which they were borrowed. In this sense metaphors are carriers of meaning and images from one context to another. (p. 274)

When metaphors become separated, as they often do, from the historical and cultural context in which they originated, their structural roots are hidden (Bowers, 1980). The resulting literal interpretation or 'reification' of metaphors is dangerous, because the human intentionality behind them is forgotten, leaving a conception of mechanical causality in the place of a dialectical process (Berger and Pullberg, 1964; Bowers, 1980). As Taylor (1984) explains:

> A metaphor is only alive when there is a realization of duality of meaning. When there is no awareness of such duality, when the

metaphor comes to be taken literally, so that schools *do* have an output, that man *is* a mechanism, we are dealing with a dead or hidden metaphor. (p. 6)

Thus, whereas metaphors can both enhance and clarify our understanding by creating new meanings and perspectives, they can also limit, reduce, and oversimplify our sense of 'reality' in any given situation. Dickmeyer (1989) expresses concern over this reductive quality of metaphors:

The major limitation of metaphors is in their inherent simplification. Out of many interacting factors available in a system as complex as learning, we choose to highlight only a few with metaphor. (p. 152)

The links between ideology, history, metaphor, and education are taken up by Taylor (1984) when he describes work done by Hawkes (1972):

Hawkes (1972) has shown how in the 16th, 17th, and most of the 18th centuries, metaphors performed a didactic function, manifesting truths, ideas and values that would carry public assent, reinforcing rather than challenging or questioning established views of the world. The metaphors of education represent the claims made by groups to impose their own sets of meanings on experience. Metaphor is part of a linguistic code that helps to create relevance and to constrain social identities . . . within many of the groups that participate in educational discourse there are distinctive codes and patterns of metaphorical usage which in creating a shared referential literacy also serve to mark off boundaries and define conditions of membership. (p. 17)

A good example of an ideological link to metaphor can be seen in the work of playwrights such as Shakespeare, who through the characters in their plays, link black and white with bad and good, thus associating Renaissance racism with morality.

The metaphors used by various authors evoke the particular images and ideologies of teaching that underlie their own work. De Castell (1988) notes, among the wide range of images used by scholars through the centuries to describe teachers, Socrates' teacher as midwife, Dewey's teacher-as-artist/ scientist, Skinner's teacher-as-technician, Stenhouse's teacher-as-researcher, Eisner's teacher-as-artist, Greene's teacher-as-stranger, and her own teacher-as-strategist, an image she derives from comparing teaching to warfare:

Warfare — this way of seeing often, sadly, seems to aptly describe how both teachers and students feel in their day-to-day and year-to-year interaction with one another. (p. 69)

In stark contrast to De Castell's image, are Bullough's (1991) findings which indicate that many beginning teachers see teaching as a form of mothering or nurturing. He also uncovered images as diverse as teacher-as-butterfly, teacher-as-policewoman, teacher-as-chameleon, and of course, teacher-as-bitch. Joseph & Burnaford (1994a) noted with some astonishment the recurrence of the image of teacher-as-witch in fictional accounts as well as in narratives written by teachers themselves. As we shall discuss more thoroughly in later chapters, we too found many such images, including a drawing of a monstrous witchy female with long steel claws instead of fingers.

Images and Teacher Identity

In the ongoing deliberations on teachers' work and professional development, teacher identity is too often treated as unproblematic and singular in nature. It is usually taken for granted in some a priori way as an outcome of pedagogical skills or an aftermath of classroom experience (Britzman, 1992). Drawing on Goodson (1980), Elbaz (1991) notes that this way of viewing the teacher 'represents a subject who is on the one hand depersonalized, that is, essentially interchangeable with other subjects, and on the other hand static, seen as existing outside time or unchanging' (p. 7). Britzman (1992) concurs, stating that this static view unproblematically scripts teacher identity as synonymous with the teacher's role and function. But role and function are not synonymous with identity:

> whereas role can be assigned, the taking up of an identity is a constant social negotiation that can never be permanently settled or fixed, occurring as it necessarily does within the irreconcilable contradictions of situational and historical constraints. (*Ibid*, p. 42)

Britzman takes her inspiration in part from Bakhtin (1986), whose view of what he calls the 'ideological becoming of a person' reveals the perpetual incompleteness of identity. Bakhtin posits two types of discourse which clash, pushing and pulling us in opposite directions, and evoking a model of becoming that is propelled by shifting conversations and that is more circular than linear:

> There is the centripetal, or the tendency toward the norm which is embodied in authoritative discourse, and the centrifugal force, or the push against authority, the refusals, the breaks — the imaginative space — that constitute internally persuasive discourse . . . authoritative discourse demands our allegiance and is embodied in 'the word of the father, parent, teacher' . . . internally persuasive discourse is tentative, suggesting something about one's own subjectivity and something about the subjectivities and conditions one confronts. It is the dialogical relation — between authoritative and internally persuasive discourse — that allows each discourse its fluidity, constraints, and possibilities.

> The struggle for voice begins with this dialogic relation . . . (Britzman, 1992, p. 32)

'How do you *see* yourself as a teacher?' A questioning of identity necessarily involves image-making. What role do the images of teaching in popular culture silently play in colouring the voices we use to speak our identity? Margaret Mead (1951/1962) was one of the first to recognize the power of image in the media, literature, and other forms of popular culture to create our sense of what is possible, normal, usual. This sense becomes part of our identity, a view supported by Giddens (1991):

> In high modernity, the influence of distant happenings on proximate events, and on intimacies of the self, becomes more and more commonplace. The media, printed and electronic, obviously play a central role in this respect. Mediated experience, since the first experience of writing, has long influenced both self-identity and the basic organization of social relations. With the development of mass communication, particularly electronic communication, the interpenetration of self-development and social systems, up to and including global systems, becomes ever more pronounced. (p. 4)

As in the case of Hi (from the comic strip *Hi and Lois*), who couldn't remember the name of his son's teacher, but could instantly remember the name of a teacher from a television program (see chapter 1), images in popular culture can even displace personal memories (Lipsitz, 1990). Joseph and Burnaford (1994a) contend that memory often perpetuates the horrible images rather than the positive ones, thereby affecting the teaching profession in a negative way. The continued popularity of such images as teacher-as-tyrant, teacher-as-buffoon, and teacher-as-bitch, and the preponderance of negative rhymes and chants about teachers suggest that there is certainly some truth to Joseph and Burnaford's assertion. But they also acknowledge a current of progressive, positive images — 'empowered teachers . . . who celebrate their influence and creativity' (p. 18) — that counter the negative images of teaching in popular culture. As Giroux and Simon (1989b) suggest,

> Popular cultures may contain certain aspects of a collective imagination which make it possible for people to surpass received knowledge and tradition. In this sense, popular culture may inform aspects of a counter discourse which help to organize struggles against relations of domination. (p. 227)

Teachers are not merely victims of society's cultural imagery. Although they are born into powerful socializing metaphors, some of them manage to break and recreate images while making sense of their roles and forging their self-identities.

Stereotypes, Popular Culture, and Teacher Education

Many professors of Education choose their career out of the conviction that teacher education is the key to reforming the schools, hoping through their university teaching to motivate future teachers to make schools better places for children to be (Weber, 1990). By offering alternative teaching metaphors, reflective writing experiences (for example, Liston and Zeichner, 1991), and certain theoretical and practical stances, many teacher educators hope to inspire and equip their students to improve schooling in some way (for example, Cornbleth, 1987; Weber, 1990). However, confronted with the realities and complexities of university-based teacher education, education professors sometimes feel unable to combat what they perceive as firmly entrenched stereotypes and ideas about teaching.

The source of this frustration is often attributed to either the powerful and conservative influence of beginning teachers' prior beliefs about teaching, or to the even more powerful and equally conservative nature of socialization into the profession that takes place in both practicum and induction experiences (Armaline and Hoover, 1989; Campion, 1984; Giroux, 1981; Lacey, 1977; Lortie, 1975; Zeichner and Tabachnik, 1981). There is a tendency, however, to oversimplify the socializing nature of cultural imagery, reducing it to a one-dimensional bogey-man to be disdained, fought, or most often, simply ignored. As Joseph & Burnaford (1994b) recognize, contemporary understanding of teachers and teaching would be greatly informed by searching for the heterogeneity that images offer.

Relatively few scholars have focused on the importance of popular stereotypes to teacher's work and identity. Waller's (1932) classic inquiry into teacher's work, for example, still has much to offer. Waller proposed that favourable stereotypes represent the community ideal of what a teacher ought to be, and unfavourable ones represent the common opinion of what a teacher actually is. In another classic work, Mead (1951/1962) points out that the stereotypes that are prevalent in the popular culture and experience of childhood, play a formative role in the evolution of a teacher's identity, and are part of the enculturation of teachers into their profession. Referring to Lortie's work on stereotypical images of teaching, Britzman (1991) too, raises the connection between professional identity and stereotypes, saying that,

> the persistency of stereotypes does more than caricature the opinions and hopes of a community. Such images tend to subvert a critical discourse about the lived contradictions of teaching and the actual struggles of teachers and students. Stereotypes engender a static and hence repressed notion of identity as something already out there, a stability that can be assumed . . . trapped within these images, teachers come to resemble things or conditions; their identity assumes an essentialist quality and, as such, socially constructed meanings become known as innate and natural. (p. 5)

Mead (1951/1962) described the image of teacher that dominated America in the first half of this century as one of white, middle-class respectability, femininity, docility, and order. In reviewing 20th-century images of teaching in North American popular culture, Joseph and Burnaford (1994a) found many similar images. Are today's stereotypes different from yesterday's? It's one thing to look critically at teaching in movies, books, and television, but quite another to assess the impact these media have on people, and the sense people make of the images that bombard them. To find out more about the import of popular culture to teacher identity, to read the social markings of personal conceptions, we asked children and teachers to draw a teacher. As noted in the previous chapter, we used this activity to investigate how people 'read' the cultural text of teacher. How do children draw teachers? How do teachers draw themselves? Our collection is a suitable starting point for professional self-reflection and cross-generational dialogue between and among teachers and children.

Even a cursory analysis of drawings done by children and teachers reveals the persistent and pervasive presence of traditional images of teaching as transmission of knowledge from all-knowing teacher into empty vessel student. Reminiscent of Goodlad's (1984) study of over 1 000 American schools, the typical teacher portrayed in the pictures drawn by both teachers and children was a white woman pointing or expounding, standing in front of a blackboard or desk (see colour plate 2). We were led to conclude (as Lortie noted in the 1970s), that the traditional stereotypes described by Mead in the 1950s remain firmly entrenched in today's children (some of whom will be tomorrow's teachers) and in today's teachers (all of whom were among yesterday's children), despite the common perception that teaching methods nowadays are radically different. As Delamont (1987) has indicated, traditional teaching methods can often be found in the guise of progressive techniques:

> What counts as 'progressive' and 'traditional' has changed over the last forty years, and beneath the rhetoric all the evidence suggests that teachers value the 3Rs as much as they ever did. The idea of the teacher who ignores basic skills is very much a creation of 'traditionalists': very few such teachers have ever been found in real life . . . In summary, despite the 'progressive' *appearance* of junior school classrooms with tables, small groups and chatter, the interaction patterns are highly traditional. Most of the time the teacher is directing the class and giving out facts, monitoring silent seat work, marking books, hearing children read or doing 'housekeeping'. Only a tiny amount of a pupil's time is spent in direct contact with a teacher, and very little of what the teacher does is cognitively stretching. (pp. 11–15)

In reflecting and commenting on the pictures they drew, many prospective teachers became aware of the power that past experience and stereotypes seem to have on them. They expressed, often with consternation, their ambivalence in relation to the dominant transmission images of teaching culturally embedded in the teaching profession. The following excerpts from their journals illuminate further:

1.2. I drew my teacher very traditionally with glasses, conservative clothing, in front of a chalkboard, a woman. I don't think I was thinking about myself as a teacher but more what many of my elementary school teachers looked like. What a stereotype! . . . A picture of a teacher sitting with her class as they are actively involved in their learning would be a more appropriate 90s picture . . . *though it's kind of funny how many of the pictures drawn by my classmates resembled mine. Many other professions don't have such a strong stereotype.* (Renee, student teacher) (italics added)

1.3. When asked to either imagine or even draw a picture of a teacher, I still come up with the same figure I used to think of when I was younger. . . . *it seems like we can't completely rid ourselves of the traditional ways.* (Brigitte, student teacher) (italics added)

1.4. It's funny how I believe myself to be non-traditional yet here was this teacher standing at the front of the class. I realize there was some factors that made me draw this way but I could have attempted to draw the scene I had wanted to do at first. Maybe this is the true reflection of any teaching — *maybe I want to break away from this traditional role I know so well but for some reason I can't.* (Carmen, student teacher) (italics added)

It is one thing to utter the word 'teacher'; it is quite another to struggle 'to name what it is to be a teacher' (Provenzo *et al.*, 1989, p. 552). Drawing, like writing, often entails the articulation or interrogation of self-identity. The following comments show that many student teachers were aware of a connection between drawing and professional identity:

1.5. Well, first of all, I drew a picture of myself . . . I think it is important to think of myself as a teacher because it is more than a 9–5 job (or 8–3). A teacher is a role model all the time. (Suzie, student teacher)

1.6. I then firmly decided that this (drawing) would be teacher X, not me, so I would not give him light-coloured hair or a beard. But then, I thought, how can I become a teacher if I don't even picture myself as a teacher? One must think positively; so, since I'm going to be a teacher, I drew me. (Stephen, student teacher) (see colour plate 10)

Like Bullough *et al.* (1991), we found that some beginning teachers resist the pressures to conform to an institutionalized teaching role and succeed in establishing a productive and coherent teaching self and concomitant style. Rather than accommodate, these teachers seek to recreate the situation. From the perspective of schema theory (Rumelhart, 1980), beginning teachers inevitably pick and choose what they will respond to in teacher education. Drawing on their past experience, they seek first and foremost confirmation of what they assume to be true about themselves as teachers and about teaching. When these views prove faulty, as they often do during student teaching, beginning teachers must find a way to adjust to the situation, to make what Lacey (1977) labelled an 'internalized adjustment' by using various coping strategies aimed either at self-preservation (Rosenholtz, 1989), or at reframing the situation. In so doing, they may develop in directions quite different from those predicted by the widely discussed progressive-traditional shift (Zeichner and Grant, 1981), and in ways quite at odds with those often sought by teacher educators (Bullough, 1991). As Anderson (1977) suggests,

> the more fully developed a schema, the less likely it will be to change
> . . . individuals will go to great lengths in order to maintain a strongly
> developed schema — and related conception of self as teacher —
> such that apparent inconsistencies and counterexamples may be easily
> assimilated. . . . People whose important beliefs are threatened will
> attempt to defend their positions, dismiss objections, ignore counter-
> examples, keep segregated logically incompatible schemata. (pp.
> 425–429)

Although most of the images of teachers in the drawings evoke a model of teaching-as-transmission, (see colour plates 2, 8 and 11), our collection also includes symbolic pictures that form a counter-text of progressive ideals, reminding us that there is also a tradition of alternative images entwined in the mainstream cliches that capture the attention of scholars, teachers, and students. The teachers' journal entries suggested that those who drew alternative images were using the drawing activity to articulate or recognize their own ambivalence in relation to dominant images of teaching embedded in our culture. Some of them consciously questioned their own identity by acknowledging, interrogating, and protesting certain stereotypes, indicating their awareness of other views of teaching:

1.7. Why is that I don't have a board nor alphabet (in my drawing)? It is supposed to be a first grade class. No alphabet? This is where I ask myself questions. There are teachers who put them up and there are others who don't think alphabets are necessary in a classroom. Who is right? (Joan, student teacher)

Others voiced ideals and aspirations, glimpses of who they would like to become:

1.8. The fear of my first image of 'the teacher' drew me to this drawing (like a rebound I suppose). Middle-aged, polyester-suited,
greasy-haired men in green holding a pointer just fill me with
fear. This drawing, in contrast, is my idealistic view. The teacher
is equal to the students and shares with them at their level . . . my
drawing, however hokey and unrealistic it may be, is likeable —
at least I like it. It has a lot in it of what I hope to be. (Vicky,
student teacher) (see colour plate 3)

Although these preservice teachers tried to use the drawings as an opportunity to symbolize the more transformative or child-centred approaches to
teaching to which they had been exposed during their teacher preparation, we
see how problematic it is even for self-aware professionals to forge new identities by modifying images that they have held all their lives — images that are
rooted in both the mythology and the reality of teaching. As Provenzo *et al.*
(1989) imply, teacher identity can be seen as a tension between the expected/
desired and the experienced.

Perhaps certain stereotypes persist because they still have a firm base, not
only in our imaginations, but also in our actual experiences of schooling and
teacher education. For example, many of the third-year preservice teachers
indicated that their actual student teaching experiences only served to reinforce traditional images (see also Liston and Zeichner, 1991; Zeichner and
Tabachnik, 1981). Perhaps most people draw a white woman standing in front
of a classroom pointing at the board because that still is the typical Western
elementary school experience lived by today's children and teachers. This
experience naturally colours perceptions of teacher identity and teaching as a
career.

The direct connection between lived experience and the portrayal of teachers was further supported by a particular grade one class-set that stood out
markedly from the drawings done by other children (see colour plate 4). Of
all the classes, these children submitted the highest percentage of non-traditional depictions of a teacher (over 30 per cent) and the highest percentage of
'happy' faces. The teachers in this set were consistently drawn playing beside,
rather than lecturing in front of the children, and were often the same size as
the children. A visit to their classroom revealed a non-traditional, whole language approach and team teaching. This finding suggests that when children
are taught with alternative models, these non-traditional experiences sometimes do find their way into drawings. There is thus a real possibility that the
stereotypes that dominate most of the drawings are not only vestiges of a past
visual shorthand to represent teaching, but are also reflections of children's
actual schooling experiences.

Our professional rhetoric tends to put a positive value on progress and
change: whatever does not change is seen as stagnant and stultified, rather
than simply enduring or stable. However, as Elbaz (1991) provocatively suggests, the persistence of images from the past is not necessarily bad:

> The traditions of the school and the culture are a source of authority for what the teacher does and says. I believe that the place of tradition in teacher thinking is a matter we have tended to treat poorly. When a teacher tells us of a particular innovation 'that won't work in my school', we are likely, as educators interested in progress and improvement, to hear this as the voice of teacher conservatism. However, it is just as likely to be the expression of the teacher's tacit understanding of school tradition and culture. I believe our difficulty in finding a place for tradition in our own conceptualizations of teacher thinking has to do with the conceptual maps we have ourselves acquired from liberal theories of education according to which progress and change based on dispassionate criticism of the outmoded ways of the past are unquestioned goods, and the traditional is seen as equivalent to the conservative and the archaic. (p. 14)

It is understandable that the teaching profession would want to distance itself from many of the stereotypes and images of teachers and teaching with which it is saturated. But it is necessary to first uncover and face the pervasive images that might be curtailing our ability to truly integrate new views of teaching into personal philosophies and practice. We contend that an insistence on reaching a single and definitive interpretation of the stereotypes and metaphors of teaching, as either exclusively conservative or emancipatory, oversimplifies lived experience, leading to a poor, or very partial reading of the cumulative cultural texts of teacher and teaching. Contradictory stories and images can help create a deeper, and more complete understanding or 'reading' of teaching. For example, in his discussion of three teachers' stories of their classroom teaching, Grant (1992) describes the reactions of a teacher, Linda, to her discovery of conflicting images embedded in her account:

> Linda was not troubled by the possible conflicting meanings of two different interpretations of her classroom. Instead, by the telling of different stories about her classroom, she was stimulated to explore and reflect upon the similarities and differences and understood that each represented alternative ways of perceiving and making sense of her classroom reality. (p. 439)

Perhaps we need to face more explicitly the probability that ambiguity, and multiple, even seemingly contradictory images are integral to the form and substance of our self-identities as teachers. By studying images and probing their influence, teachers could play a more conscious and effective role in shaping their own and society's perceptions of teachers and their work. They could ponder ways of using and even celebrating heterogeneity, viewing it not only as a problematic source of caution and critique, but also as a potential source of renewal and affirmation.

Plate 1   Fact and fantasy: Drawn by a twelve-year-old male student

Plate 2   Traditional teacher: Drawn by a nine-year-old girl

Plate 3   An ideal teacher?: Drawn by a female student teacher

Plate 4   Real teacher in imaginary setting: Drawn by a six-year-old girl

Plate 5 *Sugar and spice: An eight-year-old girl's view of her teacher*

Plate 6   *Dragon lady with breast: An eight-year-old boy's view of his teacher*

Plate 8 Prairie teacher with bun: Drawn by a female student teacher

Plate 7 Teacher's discipline: Drawn by an eight-year-old boy

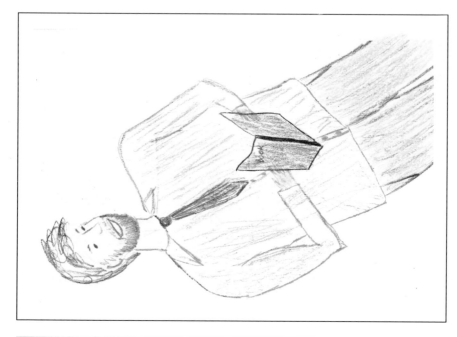

Plate 10 Clothes make the teacher: Self-portrait by a male
student teacher

Plate 9 Teacher as fairy princess: Drawn by a six-year-old girl

Plate 11   Dressed to impress: Self-portrait by a female student teacher

Plate 12 I see what you are saying: Drawn by a twelve-year-old girl

3 More Than Words: Drawing Out the Gendered Nature of Teacher Identity and Work

Drawings as Text

Evan: Why do we always have to write words? Why can't we just draw the pictures?

Teacher: Well, I like to see what you're going to write.

Julia: Why can't you just ask us? (adapted from Dyson, 1989, p. 12)

Out of the mouths of 5- and 6-year-olds, we hear a challenge to the well-established definition of texts as writing/print. The children's words of protest are brief, to the point, and important, albeit ignored by most teachers. Written texts occupy a central place in human culture, especially in Western society. We turn to them for information, knowledge, amusement, fantasy, inspiration, and confirmation. If it is written, it must be true! Many scholars, teachers, critics, and healers earn their living by making sense of what others write. In our endless fascination with writing, however, the rootedness of texts in visual imagery is neglected. The brief but typical exchange between a teacher and her young students questions the notion of 'text', calling for an extension of the term to include drawing. Work in cultural studies and media literacy has indeed begun to broaden the definition of text to include spoken language, behaviour, films, cultural artefacts (Solomon, 1988), and even universities (Schick, 1994) and shopping malls (Kowinski, 1985). That being the case, the children's plea for the inclusion of drawings-as-text seems a reasonable request.

Like writing, visual imagery has a strong communicative function. One of the hallmarks of a good written text is its ability to evoke clear, vivid mental pictures for the reader. Writing paints pictures with words, while drawings speak with lines and colours. This point is illustrated beautifully by a picture drawn by an 11-year-old girl, of a teacher reading a story to her class (see colour plate 12). The drawing features an interesting twist to the familiar cartoon technique of using words in bubbles emanating from characters' mouths or heads to communicate thought and speech. Instead of writing words to show what the teacher is saying, the girl chose instead to draw a picture in the bubble, conveying in a very creative and economical fashion the image-essence of story-telling and listening. The images evoked by the teacher's story appear to have a powerful impact, for the girl wrote on the reverse side of her drawing, 'The children's minds are flowing with ideas.'

What Drawings Can Say

Drawings have been used for decades as markers and mirrors of personal identity. Examples include well known projection tests such as the Rorshach ink-blots, the Draw a Person, and the Kinetic Family Drawing tests. Similarly, picture-drawing is, for most art therapists, a key to understanding their clients' thoughts and feelings and to helping them make sense of their life situations. Drawings offer a different kind of glimpse into human sense-making than written or spoken texts do, because they can express that which is not easily put into words: the ineffable, the elusive, the not-yet-thought-through, the sub-conscious.

Susanne Langer (1971) calls into question the Western view that ideas presented in art are less valid and important than those presented through conventional language:

> Art objectifies the sentient and desire, self-consciousness and world consciousness, emotions and moods that are generally regarded as irrational because words cannot give us clear ideas of them. But the premise tacitly assumed in such a judgment — namely, that anything language cannot express is formless and irrational — seems to be an error. (p. 91)

Much of what we have seen or known, thought or imagined, remembered or repressed, slips unbidden into our drawings, revealing unexplored ambiguities, contradictions and connections. That which we have forgotten, that which we might censor from our speech and writing, often escapes into our drawings.

Drawing can be especially revealing of the thoughts and ideas of young children, because, as the dialogue that began this chapter suggests, it comes more naturally and easily to them than conventional writing (Koppitz, 1984). Dyson (1989) observes that children's written texts often seem to be simply afterthoughts to their drawing and talking. Indeed, the consensus among researchers who have studied the development of children's writing is that drawing is their normal early form of written expression:

> Given a blank sheet of paper and an invitation to write, many young children will respond by weaving together talk, pictures, and text. (*ibid*, p. 69)

Lowenfeld and Brittain (1975) and Smith (1972) consider drawing's primary function not as representation, but as symbolic expression. Clyde (1994) urges teachers and scholars not to limit children to what is spoken or written in their efforts to make and share meaning. She describes in detail the case of Douglas, a young boy who had difficulty writing conventionally, but who meticulously maintained a pictorial 'journal' which he used as a metacognitive tool to formalize, inspect, and revise his thinking (p. 28). Goldberg (1992) argues that children's artistic expressions through music, poetry, drawing, and dance, are valuable tools that teachers can use to determine the nature of their students' understanding of facts and concepts. We agree with McNiff's (1981) assertion that

> drawing is not a process of imitating or copying the physical world, but rather of synthesizing life experiences. Art then becomes a means through which the child can communicate about those phenomena which are too complex to describe verbally, but which are being perceived and integrated into the child's organization of reality. (p. 29)

Children have control over drawing, which for them is a natural form of symbolic expression. The notion of the child-in-control is a challenge to the power that adults hold over children (Grugeon, 1993). Adults are usually considered to have an advantage over children in areas of oral and written expression, but few adults in Western societies develop a visual vocabulary and drawing skills much beyond an elementary school level, probably because drawing is not as highly valued as reading or writing (Wilson and Wilson, 1977). Thus, in print-oriented cultures, drawing in a sense puts children on a more equal footing with adults in terms of adequacy of expression. If we wish to know more intimately what children think and feel, we might begin by taking their drawings more seriously. Although art educators have been aware of this for decades, most educational research has not.

We have argued that drawings can be read as texts that reveal much of who we are and what we know. Since gender is central to identity, our interest in teacher identity leads us, in the section which follows, to explore the ways in which drawings can be read as gendered genres.

He Draws/She Draws: Probing the Gendered Genres of Schooling

One night in a cafe
Larry and Henry and I sat a whole night discussing writing.
It was the first time it occurred to me
That I had to take a path of my own,
Go my own way . . .
Because I really didn't agree with Larry's idea that you

Have to write a 'Hamlet' first, before you write well,
And I didn't quite agree with Henry either
Who was denying the personal motivation in his work —
I wanted to write in a personal way,
Very close to experience,
And what I felt to be the difference
Between what a woman has to say
And what a man has to say.
Perhaps Henry and Larry will go the same way,
But I will have to go another, The Woman's Way.
(Anaïs Nin)

Like so much of adult culture and experience, the gendered nature of preferred writing form, style, and subject matter (i.e. genre) to which Anaïs Nin alludes can be traced back to very early childhood experiences. By age 5, boys and girls tend to develop separate styles and preferences for their graphic expression. A frame from the syndicated cartoon strip *Adam*, that appears daily in many North American newspapers (see figure 1), illustrates well the gendered nature of children's drawing. A young sister and brother (approximate ages: 5 and 6), are seated opposite each other at a table strewn with crayons and paper. As each concentrate on the respective cards they are making to give to their dad on Father's Day, they have the following thoughts:

Katy: Hmmmm, Maybe I should add a few more flowers and butterflies to Dad's Father's Day card . . .

Clayton: Hmmm, Maybe just a couple more missiles and lasers blasting into Godzilla!! . . . (*The Gazette*, June 18, 1994)

Although both sexes are expressive, at this young age we can already see differences in what they draw, how they draw, and even why they draw. For example, when first grader Sarah is asked to draw a teacher, she creates

Figure 1   *Adam cartoon: He draws/she draws*

elaborate hearts, rainbows and embellished 'i's, adorning her teacher with long curly eyelashes and a ballroom gown. Her drawing reflects her admiration for the teacher; it may even have been drawn 'to please the teacher'. Andrew on the other hand, is less willing to even draw a teacher, producing instead a vivid portrait of the Power Rangers. His drawing, too, is detailed, but the detail is devoted to weapons and facial grimaces, and the lines are more angular than round.

At playtime, Sarah and her female friends play school or house, dressing up in their mother's clothes and applying make-up. This role-playing often incorporates literacy activities (Weber, 1992). In their extensive record-keeping and list-making, the girls produce samples of handwriting that contain heart-shaped dots on the 'i's, rainbow adornments, and decorative flower borders. These same visual features can be seen in the girls' playthings, such as the currently popular pastel 'My Little Ponies' figurines and other 'girls' stuff' such as Cupcake Dolls, Hollie Hobbies, Barbie dolls and the like. These cultural artefacts are a source of hours of play — a happy, chatty enactment of domestic fantasies during which dolls are dressed and undressed, taught, fussed over, taken to tea parties, and generally taken care of.

Meanwhile, Andrew and his friends are busy chasing squirrels, constructing block towers and Leggo forts, enacting dramatic war-scenes with elaborate flourishes of stick weapons, and accompanying their small action figure warriors with appropriately loud whoops and yells of attack, or perhaps they are spending mesmerizing hours in front of their television action video games, slaying monsters and killing bad guys in living technicolour. Their toys (trucks, action war figures, monsters, and the like) are brown, puce, and slime-green, with nary a heart or flower in sight. Like the girls, the boys, incorporate literacy in their play, drawing and writing imaginary monster or war comic strips, detailing battle plans, exchanging spy messages in secret code, or elaborating plans for building kites or clubhouses.

Although the above descriptions are based on real-life observations and are intended as a window into the gendered genre of children's drawing, they could also be viewed as caricatures that oversimplify genre. Our use of the term 'genre' to describe the play and drawing texts of Sarah and Andrew and their friends is modest and tentative, for as Derrida observes:

> As soon as the word 'genre' is sounded, as soon as it is heard, as soon as one attempts to conceive it, a limit is drawn. And when a limit is established, norms and interdictions are not far behind. (1980, p. 203)

Moreover, it is not our intention to present an essentialist argument which suggests that there are natural 'girl genres' and 'boy genres'. While there are many real-life Sarahs who create embellished, heart-shaped drawings, and real-life Andrews who draw endless Ninja Turtle or Power Ranger scenarios, there are also boys who hate sports and violence, but like to knit, bake, share their toys, or comfort a crying baby. There are girls who hate Barbie, Cupcake dolls and dressing up, preferring to climb trees, or play video games, hockey, or football.

Nonetheless, the pervasiveness of certain images in popular culture and advertising, the relative positions of males and females in Western society, and even the ways that adults direct boys and girls into differentiated 'appropriate' behaviour all contribute to socially constructed ways of speaking, writing, reading and playing that can be seen as gendered. For example, as Mitchell, Moonilal-Masur, and Cincik (1992), and Gilbert and Taylor (1991) observe, personal forms of writing such as diaries, journals and friendly letters are conventionally associated with girls and women. While it is true that many of the most famous diarists such as Samuel Pepys have been male, the popular culture marketing of diaries and journals has been directed much more towards girls and women. Diaries and journals have thus become a gendered genre, associated more with females than males. A further example of gendered expression is provided by Deborah Tannen (1993), who explores the gendered genres of speaking, based on the notion of report talk (male talk) and rapport talk (female talk).

It is not only children's play itself but also adult responses to the perceived gender/genre aspects of their expression that draws our attention. For example, one first grade teacher very openly admitted that she regarded girls' play as problematic. She was somewhat irritated by all the rainbows, flowers, hearts, dress-up and doll play of the girls in her class, fearing that these typically girlish activities did nothing but perpetuate stereotypes that would later lead to soap opera viewing, make-up, high heels, dressing for others, body obsession, and all of the other cultural baggage that Naomi Wolf (1991) describes at length in *The Beauty Myth*. In admitting her impatience, this teacher was only putting into words what many people think. However, such 'enlightened' concern about girls' entrapment in feminine stereotypes also displays a contempt for female popular culture and girl's play.

What is labelled as the play culture of boys is not always welcomed in grade school either. Teachers are often heard to despair of the loud, messy rambunctiousness of boys' play, especially dramatic scenarios involving pretend and sometimes all too real violence. But adult despair over boys' play often has a different tone to it. There is a kind of 'boys will be boys' acknowledgment that it is necessary and good to be assertive and active, that violence is a 'male thing' that to a certain point has to be accepted as 'natural', that boys are more independent and should be allowed latitude. Somehow boys' play and adult male activities (boxing, wrestling, weightlifting, body-building, recreational hunting and fishing, adventure magazines, even Playboy magazines) are seen by adults as less shameful and more serious than the make-up, lace, and 'sappy' romances of the culture of girls and women. Why is that? And how does this affect society's images and perceptions of teachers, and ultimately, teachers' own views of themselves?

Penelope (1990) discusses the gendered and stereotypical nature of language, contrasting the context of speaking from a position of respect and power (male), to speaking from a position of subordination and 'needing to please' (female). As genrists such as Gilbert and Taylor (1991) also observe, it is this notion of power that is of significance to any discussion of genre. The language contained within narrative forms such as stories, oral histories, and diaries has not traditionally been the language of 'getting things done' in Western society. Consequently, certain genres such as journals, soap operas, and romances are often regarded as low in status. The culture of girls and women frequently falls on 'the other side of the line', separated from the prestige or respect afforded to canonized texts. It is not just the texts that girls and women read that are devalued; as Mitchell (1982) demonstrates in a paper entitled 'I only read novels and that sort of thing', the actual act of reading by women is not held in much regard, and many women are actually apologetic for reading fiction.

Her Teacher, His Teacher

To continue our exploration of gendered genre and teacher identity, we return now to the text of drawing a teacher.

Although nearly everyone drew a female teacher, the differences in the drawings done by boys and girls were, at times, striking. After looking at just sixty drawings (two class sets), we were able to sort through a third set and accurately guess which were done by girls and which by boys. The girls took a lot of trouble over their drawings, including elaborate textual markers (earrings, eye lashes, buttons, and textile patterns). They often seemed to identify with their female teachers, incorporating them into their own playworlds by dressing them up as dolls, fairy princesses, ballerinas, or fashion models. The colours favoured by the girls (pastel pinks, purples, yellows and greens), and the symbols of love for school and teacher that were included (hearts, bows smiles, flowers), were strongly reminiscent of the cultural toy artefacts produced for girls (My Little Ponies, Rainbow Brites, Strawberry Shortcakes, Cupcake Dolls, etc.) (see colour plate 5).

The boys' depictions of their female teachers contrasted with the girls' easy identification and admiration. Their drawings tended to be less detailed and sophisticated, which we attributed not to an inferior artistic ability, but rather to a different attitude towards the task. It was as if the boys didn't really want to draw a teacher, perhaps because they viewed teachers and teaching as 'girl stuff'. Upon examining the hasty drawing done by one of her male students, a teacher remarked:

> He is a terrific artist, and if you asked him to draw monsters, snakes, Frankenstein, or blood and gore, he would put a lot more effort into it than just these scribbles.

Traces of boys' popular culture could be found in some of their pictures too. Their choice of colours, like most of their toys, were brown, puce, dark green

Figure 2   Manly female teacher

and blue, and some dressed their teachers up as Ninja turtles, rock stars, or action comic book heroes. Perhaps a more striking and generalized feature of the boys' drawings was a very ambivalent attitude towards the female teacher. One tendency was to 'masculinize' her, to the point where she looked like a man in women's clothing (see figure 2). Alternatively, they would 'feminize' her, not as the girls had done, with decorative signifiers such as make-up and jewellery, but rather with breasts as a sexual signifier (see colour plate 6). There seemed to be a certain illicit pleasure attached to this activity, since there were signs that many had tried to erase the breasts before handing in their pictures. Only a couple of girls drew a teacher with breasts.

McNiff (1981) has observed that in their drawings, girls and boys tend to have different responses to their environments. She suggests girls feel connected physically and emotionally to their surroundings and the people in them, and are especially attracted by anything with an aesthetic or sensual appeal, whereas boys are more competitive, interested in technology, and attracted to conflict. An analysis of the drawings in our collection supports these observations, particularly those referring to girls, and also reveals further nuances of gendered textuality. Consider, for example the following comment written by 10-year-old Jeanette on the back of her picture of a teacher:

1.1. She is very worried about the trees. My teacher in the picture
      loves to save trees. She is very fussy about clean-ness. She loves
      to be clean. (Jeanette, 10)

Commenting on the social caricatures assigned to teachers, Britzman (1991, p. 5) remarked that many of the stereotypes commonly associated with women teachers 'reveal a disdain for the teaching profession's female roots'. Some of the boys' attitudes towards the drawing exercise seemed to suggest such a disdain, an unconscious belittling of a profession and identity that is female, and obviously 'not theirs'. Perhaps, however, they were simply feeling free to 'rebel', to display the teacher in a less flattering light, or to take less seriously a teacher-assigned task, in comparison with the 'please the teacher', compliant attitude often attributed to girls (Robertson, 1992). As Best (1983) observes in her study of gender in the elementary classroom, girls are much more likely to be 'in tune' with their (usually female) teachers, and to seek their approval. The boys, on the other hand, tend to seek the approval of their peers, such that teachers are less central to their school experiences. Rather than identifying with or admiring their female teachers, many boys seemed to feel ambivalent or negative towards them.

Because the overwhelming majority of elementary teachers are women, what we were actually doing in gathering the drawings was, in a sense, asking girls to draw someone of the same sex and boys to draw someone of the opposite sex. For the girls, drawing a teacher meant drawing a powerful female figure in their lives, someone who often inspires fantasy, desire, love, or reverence — hence the preponderance of images of teachers dressed as princesses or surrounded with hearts. For the boys, on the other hand, the task usually involved drawing a woman who has power over them, some version of woman-in-charge-of-boys. Perhaps this is what underlies some of their half-hearted portrayals, monster teachers and 'male women'.

Women with power may be perceived as threatening by some men, who throughout history have devised certain methods of deflecting this power. One such method is mockery. Consider, for example, the image of teacher-as-witch. As Joseph and Burnaford (1994a) note, the metaphor of teacher-as-witch is strongly recurrent in fictional accounts and narratives of teachers (pp. 3–25). Many of the boys who drew monster teachers may simply have been availing themselves of a wealth of negative images and attitudes towards women that are still very much alive in contemporary popular culture.

The issue of teacher power in the classroom is an important one for children, for as scholars such as Walkerdine (1990a) and Davies (1989) point out, there are few legitimate places of female power outside the home in our society to which young children are privy. It was interesting to see the ways in which the children played out this female power in their drawing-texts: In the majority of the girls' drawings, it seemed a benign power, one exercised through a loving but firm influence and harmonious classroom relations. When harmony was disrupted, it was attributed to boys' misbehaviour (see colour plate 7). For example, many of the drawings done by both girls and boys featured names of boys 'blacklisted' on the chalkboard for not doing home-work or misbehaving. No girls' names figured on these lists. Several pictures, most but not all of them drawn by girls, depicted teachers reprimanding boys or ordering them to behave. Not a single picture in 600 portrayed a teacher disciplining a girl. There thus seems to be some consensus among children, boys as well as girls, that it is natural for boys to resist and for girls to identify with the power that female teachers exert over their students.

> Girls are . . . able to be powerful in the way that they see women being powerful. To the extent that mothers are perceived by children as powerful, and to the extent that girls see the mother as the only powerful position to which they can legitimately make any claims while constituting themselves as female, then playing at domestic games must have a deep fascination for them. (*ibid*, p. 78).

As the next section shows, one of the few roles of power to which young girls seem to aspire is that of teacher.

Identifying With Teachers: A 'Girl' Thing?

The process of learning to teach begins much earlier than the moment one decides to become a teacher (Britzman, 1991). Indeed, as Weber (1992) re-ports, a natural part of young children's (especially girls) dramatic role play includes playing 'school'. Bullough (1991) shows the direct connection be-tween childhood play and adult teachers' self-identity, quoting a woman who wrote:

> Teaching is in my blood. It's what I always wanted to do . . . I've been interested in teaching ever since I was a child, when I would hold make believe school in our family room. My two younger brothers would gather up the neighborhood children every week and would bring them over to our 'classroom'. I taught my two brothers and some of the other kids how to read and write a little bit before they even entered kindergarten. I put together a workbook made up of construction paper and staples. I made up games, stories, and cross-word puzzles. My pretend schoolhouse lasted a couple of summers, until I was in the fifth grade. (p. 46)

Walkderdine (1990) suggests that the centrality of teachers and schooling in the lives of young girls allows girls to become 'knowers' and even 'teachers' as part of regular classroom discourse. She recounts, as an example, a vignette about Sally, a bright primary aged girl, who was 'teaching' another girl by helping with her schoolwork in a teacherly way. It is thus not surprising that in several of the comments the girls made about their drawings of teachers, we could see that they projected themselves into their pictures not only as themselves (i.e. as students), but also as teachers. Some of them were quite conscious of this, telling us of their aspirations to become teachers some day. One girl, for example, wrote on the back of her drawing (a traditional portrayal of a teacher):

> 1.2. This teacher is teaching her class how to measure. Some are eager and some don't understand. I really enjoyed this activity [drawing a teacher] because that's what I would like to be when I grow up. (Sophia, 12)

Further, many of the girls' explanations of their drawings were from a teacher's point of view. Consider, for example, the following comments written on the reverse sides of pictures of teachers:

> 1.3. There once was a girl who became a teacher. She loved kids. Her favorite subject was math. She had eighteen girls in her class and twelve boys. She had thirty kids in her class. It was the first day back to school. She was getting all new students. She was so happy when the kids came in they picked a desk. The teacher said welcome to grade 2. The kids had such big smiles on their faces and so did the teacher. (Jennifer, 10)

> 1.4. In my picture 'my teacher' is teaching math. She is specifically teaching angles. The child on the right (a boy) doesn't care what is going on yet the other child (a girl) is paying a lot of attention. I decided to draw this because I see this in every class. (Marissa, 11)

It seems probable, then, that before they leave their childhood behind, many girls have already assimilated the images of teachers' actions, work, and appearance into their self-identity-as-female. Perhaps the boys too have incorporated 'female' into their conception of who teachers are, of who can teach elementary school. In terms of male self-identity, 'Teacher' might thus initially be part of what they are not, something against which they can identify their maleness. Although this situation might change in high school where male teacher role-models are found in greater numbers, our contention is that early childhood memories and images leave indelible traces that are incorporated into adult identity. Further, given that the development of identity during adolescence often involves a rebellion against authority figures, the opportunities for males to identify positively with teachers seem few, in comparison to girls who have at least the first twelve years of their lives.

Anyone whose race, social class, or background does not correspond to prevailing images of teachers, may also define 'teacher' as 'someone not like me'. As the next section will show, imagery from popular culture may serve to maintain the status quo, making it difficult for minorities and people with alternative lifestyles or values that do not 'fit' into the dominant conservative images of teacher to comfortably aspire to the teaching profession. As Trousdale (1994) observes:

> In Western countries whose student population is increasingly nonwhite, where more and more are slipping below the poverty line, and in which male student dropout rates are high it is ironic that teachers are still overwhelmingly portrayed as white, female and middle-class. (p. 212)

Teachers are Women: Gendered Aspects of Images of Teachers

The significance of women as teachers has been taken up by feminist scholars such as Walkerdine (1990) and Weiler (1988) whose work on gender in the classroom has begun to address what Luce Irigaray (1993) would describe as a 'sexuated space'. The overwhelming majority of teachers in the drawings done by both boys and girls, children and student teachers, were female. This is not surprising, given that the majority of primary and elementary teachers in North America are women (Gaskell and McLaren, 1987; Grumet, 1981). The student teachers (most of them also female) noticed and commented on the association they automatically tended to make between 'teacher' and 'woman':

1.5.   I drew my teacher like this because she looks like all of the elementary school teachers I had. Most of my teachers have been women and most of them wore skirts. (Genevieve, student teacher)

1.6.   Most of my teachers were female, except for the physical education teacher who was the requisite male. (Ellen, student teacher)

Even men who intend to become teachers themselves may automatically associate 'teacher' and 'woman'. For example, Stephen, one of the few men enrolled in our sample of beginning teachers, made the following comment:

1.7.   What sex is a teacher? I might have originally drawn a woman, *since my brain tells me that a teacher is female*, but I wanted also to strike a blow for male equality. I wanted to make a conscious effort to overcome stereotypes (how else are we to get around these except by conscious effort?). (Stephen, elementary student teacher) (italics added)

The majority of the teachers portrayed in the student teachers' drawings were not only female, but also a certain 'kind' of female. A significant number wore long skirts, with their hair pinned back in severe buns, evoking the stereotype of an 'old maid' (see colour plate 8). This image seemed to be strongly rooted in both childhood experience and cultural history, as the following excerpts from their logs indicate:

1.8. I drew my teacher very traditionally with glasses, conservative clothing, in front of a chalkboard, a woman. I don't think I was thinking about myself as a teacher but more what many of my elementary school teachers looked like. What a stereotype! (Margaret, student teacher)

1.9. I must embarrassingly admit that my view is shaded by stereotypes. It's funny because a part of me still sees a teacher as a woman in a long prairie dress in a one room school house somewhere in the country. She is extremely traditional and proper, as well as warm and sensitive. This is quite peculiar since it does not match my own liberal education nor my view of my own teaching persona. Now that I think about it, it bothers me that I have this image. (Louise, student teacher — see colour plate 8)

Images from the past are often in contradiction with those of the present, creating an uncomfortable dilemma or dissonance in teachers' minds. The drawings are laced with counter-texts, expressing the flux of teacher identity. They reveal prevailing conservative as well as radical social conceptions of teaching and ambivalent attitudes towards teachers and women. The comments used throughout this chapter illustrate that many student teachers are making a conscious effort to combat traditional images which are obviously still very powerful and prevalent within the profession.

As we shall be exploring in the remainder of the book, the images that shape our views, that in a sense rewrite what our own schooling experience may tell us, seep unnoticed into our unconscious musings through our interaction with popular culture. Trousdale (1994), for example, examines how American schoolteachers are portrayed in children's books and writes:

Female teachers come in a variety of body types. Some are slim; some are of average build; others are plump. Some are young; some are middle-aged; others are older. Some are arrayed in frilly, feminine fashions; others wear more tailored clothing. The only characteristic common to the female teachers who are given positive treatment is that they smile. They smile *a lot*... The two male teachers who are presented in a positive light are young, and they dress casually (Schwartz, 1988; Tester, 1979)... Neither, however, is the constant smiler that we see among the positive female teachers. (p. 206)

What does a smile signify? Surely the female teachers' smiles are intended to indicate good will, a lack of threatening intent. But a smile,
as it is often unconsciously practiced by females, also signifies a lack
of threat that may be interpreted as a submissive attitude, a desire to
please. Why do the male teachers not need to smile so continuously?
Does this reflect male and female socialization, and if so, what does
it mean for the role of female teachers both in the classroom and in
the larger contexts of school and society? (p. 207)

Trousdale goes on to report that the majority of female teachers depicted in
the sample of books had no name, whereas in contrast every male teacher had
a name:

This namelessness indicates that female teachers are perceived as lack-
ing in individuality and force of personality . . . One might suppose that
this namelessness suggests that the teacher archetype is so familiar that
she needs no name; we know her, named or not . . . Yet no archetypal
teacher prevails among the nameless ones. (p. 209)

Several questions could be raised by the fact that in many countries,
teaching young children is something that white, middle-class women do. For
example, are the traditional models an example of women taking up what
used to be a man's job on the implied condition that if they want to keep that
job, they must teach as men used to (i.e. traditionally)? Or, alternatively, do
certain traditional images simply reflect the way women want to teach? Like
soap operas, romance novels, storytelling, Barbie dolls and other elements of
girls' and women's popular culture that have been vehemently dismissed as
trash, perhaps traditional models of teaching have also been too quickly and
completely dismissed.

Teachers' Work

If we want to understand how teachers make sense of their work —
to acquire an empathetic understanding from within — we believe that
we must explore an artistic form of image that can grasp and reveal
the not always definable emotions. (Efron and Joseph, 1994, p. 55)

What do teachers do? What do they look like in action? Although we have
looked in detail at the differences between males and females on the drawing
task, it is equally important to point out that there was a broad consensus
about the structure of teachers' work evident among males and females, children
and teachers alike, a consensus even on some of the contradictory countertexts
present in the drawings. As we saw in the previous chapter, teachers were
usually portrayed by everyone as a smiling white woman standing in front of

the classroom by a blackboard or desk, talking and pointing. But the drawings also reveal a good deal more than that, sketching for us how people perceive the structure and nature of teachers' work.

Teachers Maintain Order, Suppress Pleasure, and Promote Work

The stereotypical images of obedience and order are handed down through popular culture from generation to generation. (Joseph and Burnaford, 1994, p. 6) The 'successful' teacher ... does not awaken students' intelligence. Such teachers value order; order is what they strive for, what they are paid for. (*ibid*, p. 16)

Both teachers and students implicitly understand two rules governing the hidden tensions of classroom life: unless the teacher establishes control there will be no learning, and, if the teacher does not control the students, the students will control the teacher ... A teacher-centred approach to learning is implicitly sustained since this myth assumes that students are incapable of leadership, insight, or learning without a teacher's intervention. (Britzman, 1986, p. 449)

The drawings contain a multitude of images that reinforce the common belief held by both teachers and children that an important part of a teacher's job is to control student behaviour and maintain order in the classroom. Colour plate 7, for example, shows a female teacher telling a boy to sit down. On the ever-present chalkboards at the front of these classrooms, many drawings feature lists of classroom rules, or lists of offenders (usually boys). Children's desks, when they figure in the drawings, are in orderly rows. Teachers' desks are usually adorned with neat piles of books and paper, with everything in its place. As the following excerpt from a teaching log indicates, the cultural markers of schooling such as desks, chalkboard, and pointer symbolize teacher authority and control:

1.10. The first two things that came to my mind when asked to think of a teacher were a desk and a board. A teacher can't be a teacher without these two. I guess I made the desk quite big because it is that that gives the teacher some power and control ... (Arlene, student teacher)

Fine (1989) believes that even today, 'the typical classroom still values silence, control, and quiet' (p. 160). The individual teacher's ability to control the class seems to be a preoccupation of both teachers and students. Indeed, for students, this structural feature of the teacher's work often appears as an extension of the teacher's personality (Everhart, 1983; Payne, 1984; Waller,

1932). Thus, for example, both children and adults defined a 'nice' teacher as someone who could exercise this control without yelling. One 11-year-old girl, for example, wrote on the back of her drawing of a teacher: 'The students really like their teacher because she doesn't yell too much.' As Aronowitz (1989) maintains,

> school is an activity, from the point of view of all its participants, that systematically denies pleasure; in fact, one of its most valuable features from the view of the dominant anticulture is its regime of discipline and the conversion of play into labor. (p. 202)

This negation of pleasure doesn't happen the minute young children enter school. Some drawings of teachers done by kindergarten and grade 1 children contrasted vividly with all the other pictures. Many of the youngest children drew their teacher outside of the schoolhouse, surrounded by sunshine, rainbows, and bright green grass. Teachers are portrayed skipping rope, walking outside, standing beside rather than in front of their smiling students. Although these pastoral representations may simply be characteristic of young children's drawings, they might also point to fundamental differences between pedagogical practices favoured by many teachers of very young children (for example, play centers, free-play time, freedom of choice of activity), and the work-discipline models that characterize elementary and high school pedagogy. By the upper elementary grades, the following sorts of comments on the drawings prevailed:

1.11.   Mine is about a teacher calling the class to attention and a bully is beating up a nerd and another nerd is telling the teacher that he is beating up his friend. And Tom, Dick, and Harry have to give in 5.00$ tomorrow. The teacher is getting mad! (Ray, 11 — see figure 3)

1.12.   In my picture 'my teacher' is teaching math. She is specifically teaching angles. The child on the right (a boy) doesn't care what is going on yet the other child (a girl) is paying a lot of attention. I decided to draw this because I see this in every class. (Marissa, 11)

As we saw in the teaching log excerpts quoted earlier, some of student teachers seem to yearn for a practice that could include pleasure and play, but despair, because 'the system' militates against this possibility. Our picture collection offers little support for democratic or play-based models of teaching. In fact, it confirms the ironic situation identified by Spring (1992) that 'the supposed protectors of democracy, the public schools, do little to promote a political culture that would help a democratic society survive' (p. 5). Moreover, although children do not seem to conceive of their teachers as people with a

Figure 3   Calm down class: Classroom discipline

life outside of school, they do seem to think that teachers are the way they are because of their personal characteristics. There was little in the children's comments to suggest an awareness of institutional constraints and expectations, or sociopolitical demands and influences. As Britzman (1986, p. 445) observes:

> To students, school hierarchy looks more like a teacher's personal decision than a structural feature of the school (Everhart, 1983; Payne, 1984). For students and teachers who remain in the same classroom day after day, the classroom does indeed take on the appearance of a separate and private world. Its relationship to school structure is taken for granted and thus becomes invisible, as do the underlying values of social control, hierarchical authority, and knowledge as external to the knower . . . The teacher's classroom appearance, however, as autonomous, charismatic and in control (Denscombe, 1982), tends further to cloak school structure by glorifying individual effort. But while the classroom represents the teacher's mandated authority, it also represents the teacher's isolation. Within the culture of teachers, the combination of isolation and an emphasis on the value of autonomy functions to promote an 'ethos of privacy'. (Denscombe, 1982, p. 257)

The organized, work-centred focus of the teaching task is frequently represented in the drawings by homework assignments written on the chalkboard or student workbooks piled high on the teacher's desk for correcting. The children's interviews and written comments emphasized the importance of 'right answers' in school, pointing to an underlying epistemological model of teaching as transmission, and knowledge as memorizing or knowing how to arrive at the 'right' answers of a fact-driven tradition. With or without a pointer, the teacher's job, according to both children and student teachers, is to point the way to the right answers, which teachers must explain, and children must remember. Consider, for example, the following:

> 1.13. The teacher is give a spelling bee to the class. Sara is stumbling on a word. The teacher helps her with the word. Sara still does not know the word. The teacher said go sit, you don't know your words. (Alicia, 10)

> 1.14. My picture is about a teacher correcting math on the board. She is correcting times tables and she is happy that everybody got everything right. (Laura, 9)

Good Teachers Nurture?

As Joseph and Burnaford (1994) remark, popular culture is inundated with images of teachers as paragons as well as images of villains. Traditional transmission images of teaching do not automatically mean that teachers are stern, witch-like, bitchy, or authoritarian (although a significant number of drawings, particularly those drawn by adolescents and adults do indeed make that connection). Many of the drawings in our collection show a teacher smiling and imply in various ways that students have an affection for their teachers, and are aware of the humanistic or relational side of teacher's work:

> 1.15. All the students like her as a teacher. If she retires all the kids will be very sad. She is like a mother to the kids. When the kids graduate they are going to come back and see her teach her class. (Glenda, 11)

Kind, nurturing images of teachers occurred most frequently in the drawings and comments of elementary female students and preservice female teachers, consistent with the idealized portraits of teachers in much of the popular culture marketed exclusively for girls. In response to our question 'is a teaching job better suited to men or to women', we received a variety of comments, as the following excerpts from a grade 5 class indicate:

> 1.16. I think it should be women, because they're nicer. But then men can be nice. (Tanya, 10)

1.17. I think it is better for elementary for women to teach and high school for men to teach. You have to be more kind and patient for elementary school. You have to be more strict in high school and men are more rough. (Martine, 10)

1.18. Men don't suit teaching because they can be very rough. Women is (sic) much better to teach because they understand kids better because they're probably a mother. (Elizabeth, 10)

1.19. Women are better because they are not that strict. (John, 10)

These comments suggest that although they acknowledge that a teacher can be male or female, both girls and boys generally think that women are especially suited to be good elementary teachers because they are kind and nurturing. The children's perceptions thus reflect and even contribute to the reality that women are more present in the elementary schools than in the high schools, and they reinforce the stereotypes that feminine 'softness' is required for elementary teaching and male 'toughness' is desirable to handle the reality of high school teaching.

Teaching Means Teaching Maths: Gender, Power, and Desire

There once was a girl who became a teacher . . . Her favorite subject was math . . . She began to teach math. She asked one of her students to do the problem on the board. He got it right. (Jennifer, 10)

Classrooms may look different today from the way they did in the 1940s or 1950s, but children are expected to work alone on a maths or language task very similar to those offered their mothers and grandmothers. (Delamont, 1987, p. 15)

Maths was the subject most often portrayed in the drawings. Numbers and maths symbols are among the most frequently used symbolic markers used by both children and adults to draw a teacher. Maths seems to be perceived as *the* school subject that speaks directly to the purpose of teaching. It's as if the ability to interpret the code/language of maths is a central part of what makes a teacher a teacher, which leads to an interesting paradox: Women are but a tiny minority in the community of mathematicians. Girls are considered to be maths-phobic, despite a growing number of studies that indicate their achievement is roughly equal to boys' in the subject. And yet, women are the ones who introduce both boys and girls to maths, women who, because it's their job, are teaching maths in the elementary schools. Both the boys who may grow up to love maths and the girls who seem more likely to grow up indifferent to it are initiated into the subject by female teachers. Of course, that's

Figure 4 *Teacher's favourite subject*

simply because there are so few men teaching in elementary schools. The following quote suggests that if men were there, they'd probably be perceived as doing a better job of it:

> 1.22.   One day a teacher and her class were learning about dividing. Her class just could not get it. But then the principal walked in and he explained it and they all understood. (Lucy, 10)

Being able to solve the riddles of maths is empowering, hence, perhaps, the enduring image of maths as 'male', evidence to the contrary. It is fascinating to see how so many girls seized on the magical status maths imparts in their romantic portrayal of teachers.

Teachers showed up in a significant portion of the girls drawings as Barbie look-alikes, beautiful fairy princesses (see colour plate 9), elegant jewellery-bearing 'ladies', femme fatale fashion mannequins, and, among older girls, as young and trendy, or 'cool'. Bedecked in these fashions, these female teachers were nonetheless often portrayed standing in front of a blackboard filled with maths symbols and traditional homework assignments talking to rows of children. These drawings could be viewed as texts of a particular fantasy: 'What if a beautiful fairy princess were teaching mathematics?' — not a new order of mathematics, or mathematics in collaborative working groups, or images of eco-mathematics, but conventional mathematics. We see in these pictures a fanciful intertwining of traditional male authority and female beauty, a yearning of sorts to be feminine AND powerful. In a similar fashion, some boys expressed fantasies of increased power, imbuing their teachers with superhero strength and omnipotence. These and other desires were expressed especially by the ways in which children and adults 'dressed' their teachers. The significance of adornment and teacher appearance in everyone's drawings will become clearer in chapter 4. Chapters 5, 6 and 7 will delve more deeply into the images of teaching in popular culture, revealing how the images we have seen in the drawings reflect many aspects of how teachers are presented not so much IN School as OUTSIDE of school.

4   Clothes Make the Teacher?
Adornment and Identity

Clothes are inevitable. They are nothing less than the furniture of the mind made visible. (James Laver)

Beware of all enterprises that require new clothes. (Henry David Thoreau)

If I were able to choose one book from among the many that will be published during the 100 years after my death, do you know which one I would choose? No, I would not select a novel from this library of the future, nor a history book (when a history book is of interest, it is also a novel). No, my friend, I would select a fashion magazine to see how women will dress a century after my demise. And those bits of fabric will tell me more about the future of humanity than all the philosophers, novelists, commentators, scientists, and scholars. (Anatole France)

Tomorrow is your first day of teaching at an inner city school where you have never taught before. Or perhaps your posting is in some unfamiliar posh public school ('private school' in North America). What question races at least once through your mind?

You are an experienced teacher or university professor. You are invited to give a talk to a group of feminists, or unionists, or parents, or politicians, or psychologists, or social workers. What question sends you rummaging through your wardrobe? 'What should I wear?'

No? Don't be ridiculous, you say? That question never crosses your mind? You never give your clothing a second thought. You couldn't care less what you look like. After all, you are a teacher or lecturer or scholar — it's what you say that counts, right? You are neither materialistic nor preoccupied with fashion; you are too intellectual, or serious, or busy, or altruistic to bother with such matters. You'd simply wear 'your usual' — maybe the same old shirt and jeans you always wear.

Even if, in fact, you end up wearing that same old outfit, if you deny any concern about your appearance, the likelihood is that you are unaware of how you operate, of how much your appearance DOES matter to you. That same old outfit constitutes your personal choice or at the very least, your lack of opportunity or ability to choose. According to Goffman (1959), dressing is our way of presenting ourselves to the world, a statement we make whether we recognize it or not. Our identification with and participation in a social group always involves body language and adornment (Lurie, 1981). Moreover, the communicative power of our appearance may far surpass our communicative intent (Buchler, 1955). Writing from a psychoanalytic perspective, Flugel (1930) goes so far as to label much of human clothing as a neurotic symptom. As Lurie (1981) points out,

> we should not be surprised to find in the language of clothing the equivalent of many of the psychological disorders of speech . . . the repetitive stammer of the man who always wears the same jacket or pair of shoes whatever the climate or occasion; the childish lisp of the woman who clings to the frills and ribbons of her early youth. (p. 35)

But then, happily, we can take comfort in the realization that there are exceptions; some people are so verbally eloquent that they can comfortably ignore social habits and pressures regarding dress.

> Like any elaborate nonverbal language, costume is sometimes more eloquent than the native speech of its wearers. Indeed, the more inarticulate someone is verbally, the more important are the statements made by his or her clothes. People who are skilled in verbal discourse, on the other hand, can afford to be somewhat careless or dull in their dress, as in the case of certain teachers and politicians. Even they, of course, are telling us something, but they may not be telling us very much. (Lurie, 1981, p. 22)

In this chapter, we explore the power and meaning of appearance and dress in the images and identity of teachers. Following Schwarz (1979), we use clothing, appearance, costume, adornment, and dress almost interchangeably to refer not only to items of clothing, but to all forms of bodily modification, including glasses, hairstyles, make-up, tattoos, body decoration, jewellery, accessories, and the like. Our theoretical perspectives are derived from the anthropology, history, and semiotics of clothing. By referring to films, books, television, colour drawings and excerpts from interviews with teachers and children, we show how clothes link social expectations and cultural variations to individual interpretation and expression, and we document and analyze the significance of appearance to beginning teachers' sense of identity and to children's perception of teachers.

Clothing as Text

Why clothes? Although certain scholars favour one theory over another, there is general consensus that the historical evolution of adornment and clothing is a response to three basic needs or human motivations, what Laver (1949) has designated as: the Utility Principle (to ensure body comfort and protection); the Hierarchical Principle (to indicate social identity, one's status, job, and the like); and the Seduction Principle (to attract sexual attention and ensure the reproduction of the species). The Shame Principle, emanating from the story of Adam and Eve, has largely been discarded in light of overwhelming data that, although in some contexts dress is related to shame, the basic reason for covering the body historically has been to attract rather than discourage sexual attention (Schwarz, 1979).

It is through their communicative function that clothes are able to meet so many basic human needs. Lévi-Strauss (1963) views clothing and language as fundamentally the same phenomenon. Accordingly, Bogatyrev (1971, p. 83) proclaims the suitability of semiotics for exploring the meaning of dress: 'In order to grasp the social functions of costumes we must learn to read them as signs in the same way we learn to read and understand languages'. Lurie (1981) has written extensively and insightfully about the semiotics of clothing:

> For thousands of years human beings have communicated with one another first in the language of dress. Long before I am near enough to talk to you on the street, in a meeting, or at a party, you announce your sex, age and (social) class to me through what you are wearing — and very possibly give me important information (or misinforma- tion) as to your occupation, origin, personality, opinions, tastes, sexual desires and current mood. I may not be able to put what I observe into words, but I register the information unconsciously; and you si- multaneously do the same for me. By the time we meet and converse we have already spoken to each other in an older and more universal tongue. The statement that clothing is a language . . . is not new. Balzac, in *Daughter of Eve* (1839), observed that for a woman, dress is 'a con- tinual manifestation of intimate thoughts, a language, a symbol'. . . . Sociologists tell us that fashion too is a language of signs, a nonverbal system of communication. (p. 3)

Like verbal communication, dress is a socially determined activity. Mem- bers of a given society learn a number of speech codes — the type of language that is appropriate for any given social context. We do not necessarily talk the same way with our friends as we do with our superiors at work or school. As Lurie notes:

> The meaning of any costume depends on circumstances. It is not 'spoken' in a vacuum, but at a specific place and time, any change in which may alter its meaning . . . To wear the costume considered 'proper' for a situation acts as a sign of involvement in it, and the person whose clothes do not conform to these standards is likely to be more or less subtly excluded from participation . . . In language we

distinguish between someone who speaks a sentence well — clearly, and with confidence and dignity — and someone who speaks it badly. In dress too, manner is as important as matter. (pp. 12–13)

Generally, we unconsciously change our dress and speech codes with relative ease. As in the case of the person who claims not to care about his/ her appearance ('I just dress normally'), these communication codes are so familiar they become invisible. We may 'read' and 'write' these codes in an unthinking way, taking for granted certain past symbolic representations that have become incorporated into our interpretive filters. However, like many texts, the language of dress can often be difficult to decipher. Sometimes we don't know what words to use to best express ourselves. Not knowing what to wear or realizing we have 'nothing to wear' is like being at a loss for words, or staring in panic at a blank page. Similarly, just as we can misunderstand each other's speech, or miss the multiple layers of meaning in a written text or a work of art, we can misread what dress and appearance are saying.

Schwarz (1979) states that, more than any other material product, clothing plays a symbolic role in mediating the relationship between nature, human beings and the sociocultural environment. In dressing, we address ourselves, others, and the world. How we clothe ourselves becomes an integral part of our self-identity. How, then, do teachers dress? What are the social contexts within which they operate? How are stereotypes, memories of schooling, actual experiences, dreams, intentions, complacencies and frustrations played out through their choice of clothes?

I'm not sure, but I feel a certain pressure to be well-dressed for the classroom. Perhaps clothes do indeed make the person. (Stephen, elementary student teacher, see colour plate 10)

From the moment of birth when a baby is swaddled, oiled, or circumcised, or bound, or dressed according to a gendered colour code, dress and adornment play an important role in the social construction of the self. Like most forms of communication, dress simultaneously lends itself to individual expressions of a personal nature, connecting the individual to society while giving a unique personal twist to a shared social meaning.

Dress is a means of self-display, but also relates directly to concealment/ revelation in respect of personal biographies: it connects convention to basic aspects of identity. (Giddens, 1991, p. 63)

What else does clothing tell us about ourselves and others? Do the prevailing images and stereotypes of duty urge teachers to dress in a certain way? When drawing themselves or other teachers, student teachers paid detailed attention to clothing (see, for example, colour plate 11). The children, too, were very preoccupied with how teachers dress. In loving detail, many of them faithfully reproduced the outfits their teachers actually wore, carefully drawing in every last button and earring. This attention to appearance is not an artefact of the study design. Students do notice and comment frequently on what their teachers wear. As one teacher put it: 'If I so much as change the colour of my nail polish, they notice.' In a drawing done by a 6-year-old girl, for example, a teacher is shown skipping rope ('double Dutch') in a polka dot suit and wooden clogs (see colour plate 4). During an interview, we discovered that in real life, the teacher never skips rope with her students at school. The depiction of her clothing, on the other hand, is completely true-to-life, right down to the wooden clogs on her feet. The teacher told us that on the day the picture was drawn, she was indeed wearing a spotted outfit, and clogs that she had borrowed from her daughter, as her other shoes were wet.

When we think of teacher, or remember a specific teacher we have known, it is often the way they dress that stands out. A university colleague, for example, never forgot a rather mean-spirited male teacher who, reluctant to come to school and deal with his students, delayed getting up until the last minute, and in order 'to save time' (or so he said), would routinely slip on his clothes over his pyjamas and teach with his pyjama hems sticking out of his frumpy trousers and wrinkled shirt sleeves.

Through the depiction of clothing in their drawings, and their accompanying comments, teachers and students reveal a great deal about their pedagogical beliefs. Most often, the pictures and comments evoke an image of teaching-as-transmission and of teacher as an all-knowing role-model, a figure of traditional authority who commands respect. These views are very much in keeping with the dominant stereotypes of teachers and teaching that permeate both actual school experience (Goodlad, 1984; Delamont, 1987) and popular culture (Joseph and Burnaford, 1994b). There is a general uniformity in the somewhat dull, conservative nature of much of the teacher attire portrayed in drawings and in movies and television. Children and adults alike often draw female teachers with hair drawn back in a bun, perhaps wearing glasses and pearls, and usually a skirt of some kind (see colour plates 1, 2, 7 and 8). Although female teachers are sometimes drawn with glamorous or stylish clothes (see colour plate 11), they are more often depicted in rather shapeless, sack-like attire, like that of Miss Grundy from *Archie* comics. Male teachers, too, are drawn in nondescript clothes, sometimes a suit, usually a shirt or sweater and pants, occasionally a beard, often with heavy glasses. These male teachers are often a bit scruffy, and occasionally covered in chalk dust. The drawings thus mirror many of those funny, bumbling, nerdy, unattractive, severe, old-fashioned, or pathetic teachers in movies and television, and our memories of schooling:

> 1.1. I drew my teacher very traditionally with glasses, conservative clothing, in front of a chalkboard, a woman. I don't think I was thinking about myself as a teacher but more what many of my elementary school teachers looked like. (Margaret, student teacher)

1.2. This has always been my image of teachers — long flowing skirts, glasses, nice perfume, pearls, and coffee breath. (Caroline, student teacher)

But not all teachers in popular culture or real life fit the preceding descriptions. For example, an episode of *The Twilight Zone*, an adult science fiction television program popular in the 1950s, featured as a romantic interest, a beautifully coiffed and fashionably-dressed teacher named Miss Sloane. One of the local men in the town had this to say about her:

She does a good job of those kids, Miss Sloane. Awful pretty girl for a school marm, awful pretty. Doggone I never had no school marms that looked like that when I was a kid. All my school marms looked like they came out of a pickle jar.

There are and always have been many dramatic and colourful exceptions that provide unconventional responses to the question 'What do teachers wear?' The fuchsia shirt of the substitute teacher in the girls' book *Barnyard Battle*, the elegant, soft clingy fabrics, and draping silk scarves worn by Jean Brodie in the movie *The Prime of Miss Jean Brodie*, the impeccably tailored suits worn by Mark Thackeray in *To Sir With Love*, the real-life teacher you once had who was beautiful or handsome or fashionable or eccentric or colourful — they all momentarily rupture the image of teacher as asexual and drab, offering alternative possibilities: Teacher-as-cool; teacher-as-sex-symbol/object; teacher-as-goddess; teacher-as-hero; teacher-as-gentleman; teacher-as-rebel, and teacher-as-artist. Many of these exceptions, however, only serve to underline common social expectations that teachers will conform, and not rebel. These romantic images capture our attention because of their very exceptionality, because they remind us that this is not how things usually are. In his description of one of the teachers at a school staff meeting, Garry Jones (1991), catches himself following these stereotypical ideas:

Suzanne, all curls, ribbons, nice smells and enchantment, and a Crocus Valley Estates girl with roots in France, is always dressed to have dinner with the Queen, should she happen to arrive. She has never worn the same outfit twice, as far as we can tell, and no one has been invited to her home, giving rise to the rumour that she steps out of a page in The Fashion Magazine every morning. You wonder why she ever became a teacher, *and then you wonder why you wondered*. (pp. 61–2) (italics added)

One might wonder, because teachers are not supposed to look attractive or sexy or 'different'. They are not supposed to look aristocratic. They are supposed to reflect prevailing social standards of middle class respectability. If teachers do differ from the social norm, they are expected to differ in a more negative manner that is somehow considered more true-to life: teacher-as-spinster; teacher-as-absent-minded-bumbler; teacher-as-bossy-matron. Another description by Jones (*ibid*) reveals these social expectations at work:

> Ross McAlpine, red-faced and looking like the soft-drink can someone shook but hasn't opened, scowls in the corner. He puffed in ten minutes late without his staff-meeting binder or a pencil and is now drinking milk from the carton. Even though he wears suits they always look rumpled and baggy and slept-in and wrinkled. He has a bland wife and three bland children with forgettable faces and he drives a rusty twenty-year-old car. The children laugh at him and the parents love him because in his class they stick right to the curriculum with no nonsense and no fun but strangely enough when ex-students come to visit they always visit Ross. (pp. 62–3)

The teacher's familiar blandness is appreciated by children and parents alike, because it seems to fit an undefined notion of how a teacher should be (someone with an uninteresting appearance and lifestyle, who is equally boring and methodical in class). Teachers are keenly aware of these expectations, to such extent that they may think it wisest to meet them by dressing or 'disguising' themselves according to prevailing images. The dialectical interaction between cultural images and real-life teachers' actions can thus produce and perpetuate a sort of uniform. This point is illustrated in Quigly's (1982) account of the book *Miss Pike and her Pupils*, by Mabel L. Tyrrell, that embodies many of the changing social attitudes in the 1920s:

> Its plot is like that of certain Hollywood films in which the heroine whisks off her glasses and unalluring cardigan to reveal a beauty underneath. Miss Pike runs a small school at just the time, in the mid-twenties, when female clothes were changing from the long, baggy styles with soft, feminine hair, still worn by older women, to the brief flapper skirts and shingled hair of young girls. Dowdy Miss Pike goes in for the elderly look so that parents will think her of a suitable age to run a school and the girls will respect her, and only at the very end does she take off the disguising hat and specs, put on a modern dress and marry her pupil's father. (p. 220)

Thus, although there are numerous examples of images that rub against the grain of what teachers are supposed to look like, these exceptions are almost always presented in a context that makes then look remarkable because they are not probable or usual. The surface text of 'See what teachers should or could look like (be like)' is accompanied by a persistent counter-text 'this is not normal, this is not what to expect from most of real life'. What impact does this have on professional identity?

Pressures to Conform: Resistance and Professional Identity

The images of teaching reflect the tension or struggle between individual desires to rebel and collective pressures to conform. This is played out in many ways through the language of clothes that both links and interrogates pedagogical conservatism, gender, identity, reform, fantasy, and resistance. This struggle is particularly evident in the countertexts provided by some of the beginning teachers in their drawings and comments. For many, a preoccupation with clothing in their drawings seems to be a way of examining or fighting a stereotype, often reflecting a conscious determination not to be like certain teachers they have known. Drawing a teacher dressed 'differently' is their way of symbolically breaking with tradition or reacting against personal past experience, as the following excerpts from a teaching log illustrate:

1.3. As I was doing this picture I thought of myself as a teacher. I pictured myself dressed very comfortably and surrounded by all my children. I don't know why, but ever since I was a child, I was always afraid of teachers dressed with suits. That is why I'd like to portray a different image for my children. (Madeleine, student teacher)

1.4. I gave her nice clothes because teachers dress more casually now. As well, I made her a dark-skinned woman because people of colour are not well represented. The stereotype is 'white'. (Isabel, student teacher)

This preoccupation with appearance relates, in part, to the need to deal with social and institutional pressures on teachers to conform. Roach and Eicher (1973) point out that 'some people are constrained in their individuality in dress because their occupations have rigid dress codes' (p. 127). Through our choice of clothes and adornment, we voice our struggle to become teacher, while remaining individuals. This process is illustrated further in the comments and drawings done by the student teacher Madeleine (see excerpt 1.3.). She drew two very different pictures of herself as a teacher, one before, and one after her student teaching experience. The difference in her self-portrayals reflect the pressures and struggles with which student teachers must cope:

1.5. My second picture was a little different. I'm not with little children. I'm with fifth graders and I feel as though this is the way I have to look at my practicum school. Maybe this is the idea that I get from this school. I wouldn't say it is terrible, but that is the way they happen to dress in this school, so I also try to look like these teachers as well. But I would like to look like the first picture I drew. I feel more comfortable looking like the first teacher. That's more me. (Madeleine, student teacher)

Madeleine links her desire to be more 'herself' with how she dresses, articulating an awareness of how essential clothing is to personal self-identity. Alongside her wistful desire to be more herself, we hear her simultaneous wish to be teacher. Does becoming a teacher mean becoming less who we are, a weakening of the integrity of our self-identity? Clothing is connotative, associated with a variety of thoughts and feelings. Dress can serve to channel strong emotions and move us to act (Schwarz, 1979). Clothing can be a proclamation of resistance, a mode of innovation or becoming, a reconciliation, a desire to belong, or a surrender. Would dressing more like our 'true' selves while we teach be a way of reclaiming that part of our personal identity that becomes 'lost' in the process of incorporating professional identity?

He Wears She Wears: Control and Gender in the Pedagogy of Clothes

To be a 'man' or a 'woman' depends on a chronic monitoring of the body and bodily gestures. There is in fact no single bodily trait which separates all women from all men. Only those few individuals (i.e. transsexuals) who have something like a full experience of being a member of both sexes can completely appreciate how pervasive are the details of bodily display and management by means of which gender is 'done'. (Giddens, 1991, p. 63)

Despite assertions to the contrary, men care very much about their appearance, for basically the same reasons that women do. Clothing not only helps to reflect and construct individual identity, but also demarcates gender. Where men and women seem to differ, is in their willingness to talk openly about the subject:

Practically all the most powerful men in New York . . . are fanatical about the marginal differences that go into custom tailoring. They are almost like a secret club insignia for them. And yet it is a taboo subject . . . They don't want it known they even care about it . . . sex, well, all right, talk your head off. But this, these men's clothes! (Wolfe, 1965, pp. 256–7)

Perhaps men still deny any interest in clothing, because of its strong association with female decorativeness and vanity. However, most of the few male student teachers in our study showed a preoccupation with clothes in their comments on their drawings of teachers:

1.6.   I clothed my facsimile in shirt and tie. This was originally to be my green suit but due to my meager artistic skills it became merely a green shirt. I guess a blue tie does not go well with green and brown, but I am not colour-coordinated. Do all (male) teachers dress like this? (Stephen, male elementary student teacher — see colour plate 10)

1.7. I guess that I have some affection for the big sloppy goof I picture as teacher. He's totally human and fallible, in an endearing way that contradicts his authoritative position. Still, because he is the authority, sometimes abuses that authority, he remains the enemy, and so I'm powered by a desire to try to humiliate him, make him look foolish. He has a slightly clueless, dazed, empty expression. Not an army haircut — a bit shaggy, without really making a statement. Rolled up sleeves . . . Sweaty, stinky underarm stains. Obviously not born to wear ties. A bit of a belly but not too much; just enough to look sloppy. Teacher's salary doesn't afford gross overeating . . . Maybe jeans. Dark socks, light shoes . . . Really ugly, comfy leather-sole schlepp shoes. (Arnold, elementary teacher)

As indicated in the description above, although expectations of appearance do not seem to weigh as much in the judgment people make of male teachers, there are indeed limits which men transgress at their own risk. These limits reflect whatever style of adornment currently defines middle class male respectability.

Several of the female student teachers in our study were very appearance-conscious:

1.8. My idea of the perfect teacher has pretty much remained the same over the years. The idea is that of a person (male or female) who was always well-dressed, prim and proper with no visible faults. Hair and makeup was always perfect and well applied in women, and men would be in neatly pressed suits, matching ties and always smelling good . . . and were all-knowing . . . I suppose this rubbed off on me to some degree because when I did my first practice teaching, I found myself always going in well-dressed and made up. (Tina, elementary teacher — see colour plate 11)

1.9. I drew my teacher in this way because my past female teachers always wore long skirts or dresses, pearl necklaces, and always had this serious look on their face. (Marlene, student teacher)

1.10. Another thing that is important in my drawing is my clothes. I drew myself in my favorite 'first day' outfit. Dress is important as it helps demand respect. I am very nervous about having a grade 5 class. It is important that they respect me as a teacher, and not a babysitter, or older sister. I find that being short, and

> not looking harmful are two things that work against me, so I must dress and act in a way that demands respect. (Roberta, student teacher)

The above comments are fairly typical of the remarks made by a majority of student teachers and by quite a few teachers. They reveal that to many, clothing is not only a means of identifying oneself as teacher, but is also a pedagogical strategy in itself, a means of commanding respect and order, of establishing a serious working atmosphere, and of exerting control. For Roberta, for instance, dressing 'well' is perceived as a means of gaining students' respect and attention. She seeks a business-like seriousness or severity in attire to compensate for her short stature and nervousness. For Arnold, a sloppy nondescript style indicates a way of softening or mitigating one's sometimes abusive power as teacher. He also admits that, although he himself is a teacher, he still has a lingering image of teacher-as-the-enemy, and uses clothing in his drawing as a way of exacting a bit of teasing revenge against a symbol or stand-in for the teachers from his childhood. For Tina, a teacher has to be impeccably dressed and perfectly groomed in order to project distance, superior knowledge, and status.

The image of teachers as moral guides and upstanding members of society remains strong in people's minds, and still determines, to a large extent, occupational dressing codes. A certain type of personality is inevitably assumed to accompany a given choice of clothes. Flugel (1930) proposes a provocative taxonomy that classifies individuals into various types according to their attitudes towards clothes: the rebellious type, the resigned type, the unemotional type, the prudish type, the duty type, and the sublimated type. The duty type, especially, reflects much of the imagery of teacher dress that we found in drawings and popular culture:

> the duty type — a type in which certain features of costume (for the most part either those actually associated with uniforms or other working clothes, or those that are distinguished by a certain stiffness, tightness, or severity of line) have become symbols of work and duty. In persons of this type, the interests connected with clothes have come to represent not merely, as in the prudish type, a reaction-formation against self-display in any form, but an inhibitory tendency of a much wider kind, directed against all manifestations of 'softness' or 'self-indulgence'. With them certain kinds of clothes have indeed become outward and visible signs of a strict and strongly developed 'Super-Ego' or moral principle. Such persons are apt to draw a sharp distinction between clothes worn for work and the less severe and more ornamental garments worn for rest or recreation, and (those of them at least who are capable of relaxation) tend to 'feel different', to adopt a less stiff and rigid view of life when themselves dressed in clothes of the latter type. (pp. 97–8)

Official concern with teacher attire is not simply a relic of the past. Even today, teacher educators, like the schools, exert subtle pressures on future teachers to conform to unwritten dress codes. Work done by Cole and Knowles (1993), for example, suggests that student teachers are being realistic in worrying about attire because this preoccupation with appearance is not confined to school boards, teachers, and children, but is also evident in university supervisors. They cite the following remarks written by a student teacher about one of her supervisors:

> Dr. M. stopped by my German class the other day. I did not get much of a chance to talk to him before or after he visited. He just left his notes for me and talked to me for about five minutes after he observed me . . . What really bothered me about his observation was a simple sentence he put at the beginning of the page. He wrote: 'Leila was nicely attired'. This was his first sentence. I guess I did not expect to be evaluated by my supervisors for my clothing. I know that student teachers need to be aware of their appearance in school but it hardly seems like an issue university supervisors should be concerned about. I know that Dr. M. meant well, but it is disturbing how much emphasis is put on appearance. (p. 9)

Here is an indication that, although much prevailing university rhetoric rails against the conservatism of the school milieu, teacher educators are perhaps unwittingly doing much to perpetuate rather than change the status quo. Indeed, in some teacher preparation institutions, the supervisory forms used to evaluate student teachers still contain sections dealing with teacher appearance and demeanour.

Can a teacher like Madeleine (see excerpt 1.3.), who 'dresses comfortably', command respect and fulfil her professional obligations? Can a woman who relaxes at home in a red negligee be a good teacher? What kind of hold do traditional dress codes and stereotypes still have in people's minds and in classroom practice?

As Lurie (1981) notes, the above questions are particularly pertinent to women, whose choice of clothing (and corresponding behaviour) have been historically bound by strict social dictates:

> Attempts to limit female mobility by hampering locomotion are ancient and almost universal. The foot-binding of upper-class Chinese girls and the Nigerian custom of loading women's legs with pounds of heavy brass wire are extreme examples, but all over the world similar stratagems have been employed to make sure that once you have caught a woman she cannot run away . . . high-heeled, narrow-toed shoes . . . (are) thought provocative, perhaps because (they guarantee) . . . that no woman wearing them can out-run a man who is chasing her. (pp. 227–8)

Women were told that they looked very ugly in trousers, and that wanting to wear the pants — in our culture, for centuries, the symbolic badge of male authority — was unnatural and sexually unattractive . . . any female who appeared on a formal occasion in a trouser suit was assumed to be a bohemian eccentric and probably a lesbian. Most schools and colleges insisted on skirts for classes and in the library until the 1960s . . . At the Frick Collection Library in New York women may not be admitted unless they are wearing skirts. (*ibid*, p. 225)

Even when subversion or liberation movements lead to a broader repertoire of clothes, social context and fashion subtleties can reassert patterns of domination through dress:

The wearing of men's clothes can mean many different things. In the 30s, sophisticated actresses such as Marlene Dietrich in top hat and tails and elegantly cut suits projected sophistication, power and a dangerous eroticism . . . The Annie Hall style is a double message. It announces that its wearer is a good sport, a pal: not mysteriously and delicately female, but an easy-going, ready-for-anything tomboy type, almost like one of the guys . . . At the same time, however, these clothes convey an ironic antifeminist message. Because they are worn several sizes too large, they suggest a child dressed up in her daddy's or older brother's things for fun, and imply 'I'm only playing; I'm not really big enough to wear a man's pants, or do a man's job.' This is a look of helpless cuteness, not one of authority; it invites the man to take charge, even when he is as incompetent himself as the characters played by Woody Allen. (*ibid*, p. 229)

As women more frequently wear pants, these clothes lose their emancipatory power:

Elizabeth Stanton was right, for wearing trousers and nonrestricting clothing did not automatically provide either elevated status or greater role opportunities, particularly in occupations, for women. (Roach, 1979, p. 422)

During the writing of this book, we were inundated by the media coverage of the murder trial of O.J. Simpson, a famous American football player accused of killing his ex-wife and her male friend. To plead the state's case against Simpson, the public prosecutor, Marcia Clark was counselled to cut her hair and soften her image by abandoning the tailored dark suits she usually wears. The new soft fabrics she adopted were meant to 'motherize' Clark, to mitigate her hard lawyering for the jury. The message is that it is not acceptable to have a cold or overtly aggressive female prosecutor although this is perfectly acceptable, even expected in a man. Susan Estrich, a law professor, reportedly finds this advice wise in the context of social reality, but she also finds it offensive:

> This woman is in the business of prosecuting murderers, and the notion that she has to do it wearing pink is a stunning indictment of how far we've come in terms of equal rights. (reported by Lynda Gordov of the Boston Globe in *The Gazette*, Montreal, 14 October 1994)

When females were admitted in large numbers at the turn of the century to the elementary teaching posts once dominated by men, school boards felt obliged to exercise moral control over their bodies and their lives. This was done through dress codes. The following is an example of official school board regulations issued to all female teaching personnel in most regions of Canada and the United States. Although some of these regulations were largely ignored (especially after the First World War), they nonetheless remained official well into the twentieth century.

1   Teachers will not dress in bright colours.
2   Dresses must not be more than two inches above the ankles.
3   At least two petticoats must be worn. Their petticoats will be dried in pillowcases.
4   The teacher will not get into a carriage or automobile with any man except her brother or father.
5   Teachers will not loiter at ice cream parlors.
6   Teachers are expected to be at home between the hours of 8 p.m. and 6 a.m., unless in attendance at a school function.
7   Teachers will not smoke cigarettes or play at cards.
8   The teacher will not dye her hair under any circumstances. (Nelson, 1992)

These dress codes were an attempt to save women from themselves by imposing on them some man's romantic, if ridiculous, image of female chastity. It seems that women were not to be trusted to keep their sexuality in check or to know how to behave without being told. Women were not (are not?) considered 'grown ups' in the sense that men are. Like young children who are assumed not to have the judgment and experience to know how to dress, teachers were and perhaps still are dictated to in such a way as to make it clear that they are not fully trustworthy, that it is not they who are in control. Not that female teachers always knelt down in obedience before the many ordinances that officials directed at them (Nelson, 1992). A strong tradition of quiet, unobtrusive resistance has long been in effect. Often denied a real voice in the governance of their own supposedly 'professional' actions, teachers have often learned to smile sweetly at proposed reforms and new regulations and then quietly shut their classroom doors to do as they have always done, ignore them. Which, of course, 'proves' that they cannot be trusted and need to be even more closely regulated!

Dressing Teachers: Popular Culture, Fashion, and Fantasy

> Dress is an aspect of human life that arouses strong feelings, some intensely pleasant and others very disagreeable. It is no accident that many of our daydreams involve fine raiment; nor that one of the most common and disturbing human nightmares is of finding ourselves in public inappropriately and/or incompletely clothed. (Lurie, 1981, p. 36)

Drawings offer a wonderful opportunity to express simultaneously experiences of both reality and fantasy. Accordingly, through their drawings, many people liberated teachers from the pressures to conform to 'normal' teacher dress codes. The children often chose to dress their teachers up instead in images borrowed from popular culture. Thus, as mentioned in the previous chapter, we received many carefully executed drawings of teachers as fairy princesses in long evening gowns, standing before their blackboards wielding magic wands instead of pointers (see colour plate 9). Our collection also includes teachers dressed as Ninja Turtles, troll dolls, and witches.

We found remnants of popular images in the drawings of some student teachers as well. The following comment, for example, accompanied a picture of a teacher in a long gown:

> 1.11. It's funny because a part of me still sees a teacher as a woman in a long prairie dress in a one room school house somewhere in the country. She is extremely traditional and proper, as well as warm and sensitive. This is quite peculiar since it does not match my own liberal education nor my view of my own teaching persona. Now that I think about it, it bothers me that I have this image. (Julie, student teacher — see colour plate 8)

The drawing and comment are strongly reminiscent of the pioneer teacher Laura Ingalls from the 1970s television series *Little House on the Prairie*. Once again, a stereotypical image competes with the student's own experience and views, creating a certain amount of puzzlement and frustration.

Adolescents also turned to popular culture for inspiration for teacher costume design, especially when we invited a group of them to draw their ideal teacher. According to their drawings, the ideal teacher for teenagers is a young and stylish person who shares or empathizes with the popular culture of adolescence. Many of these ideal teachers are dressed like rock stars, replete with chains, black leather, and torn jeans. If female, these ideal teachers often resemble fashion models, dressed in avant-garde versions of the latest trend. Like the younger children, in drawing their ideal teacher, the teenagers

Figure 5   Cool dood: Teacher as a punk rocker

turned their backs on the shapeless Miss Wormwood or Miss Grundy types, preferring instead other popular images not usually associated with teachers. Such is the life of fantasy.

But it is not only fantasy that shapes and is shaped by popular culture. Our everyday, sometimes all-too-real lives are heavily influenced, at times even rewritten, by popular scripts. When the question, 'what should I wear?' pops into the thoughts of teachers and future teachers, their answer may be based not only on vague memories of teachers past, but also on the more recent and clear popular images of teachers that surround us in daily life. The majority of these teacher images in no way resemble fashion models or rock stars.

Figure 6   *Serious-looking teacher*

Popular culture, which has done so much to homogenize our life, has at the same time, almost paradoxically, helped to preserve and even to invent distinctive dress through a kind of feedback process. It is convenient for producers of films, TV programs and commercials that clothes should instantly and clearly indicate age, class, regional origin and if possible occupation and personality . . . Viewing the program and others like it, (people) unconsciously accept this outfit as characteristic; they are imitated by others who have not even seen the program. Finally the outfit becomes standard, and thus genuine. (Lurie, 1981, p. 25)

The majority of popular images of teachers reinforce either the 'serious-business' look that so many real-life teachers adopt or a sloppy, dowdy look that invites indifference, derision, or pity. Both styles reinforce an image of teacher as asexual, concerned only with the mind. These images are so pervasive in television and films that they have the power to rewrite our memories, papering over the fashionable, casual, or colourful attire that some teachers really do wear, urging us to incorporate a small range of standard 'teacher' looks into our very identity as teacher. This can be viewed as liberating — we know how to dress, and we don't need to bother about it too much. We can get on with our jobs, the serious business of teaching. Alternatively, we could ask, as the student teachers did, if dressing a certain way means teaching a certain way. Business suits or skirts are not the most practical choice of attire for a discovery approach or action-based pedagogy that involves 'getting down in the muck' with the children.

Many teachers reading this chapter will not recognize themselves in much of the discussion about stereotypes of dress, and with good reason. Individual attire, like speech, is not only shaped by cultural images, but as Barthes asserts, also by our personalities. Thus, each teacher has a distinctive style that peeks through the first-glance uniformity, offering a counter-text, proclaiming a rebellious conservatism or a conservative rebellion. In dressing, we exert our right to be ambivalent, and we reveal our individual attempts to both 'fit in' and be ourselves in many ways — the comfortable, maybe even scruffy shoes worn with that tailored dress or jacket, the elegant hairdo and make-up worn with those faded baggy denims and T-shirt, the bright tie or wild plaid shirt beckoning beneath the tweed jacket, the patterned socks peeking from under the trouser legs, the jaunty cap and leather jacket hanging in the teachers' cloakroom, the velour jogging pants worn underneath the science lab coat, the lacy underwear that, although outwardly invisible, somehow changes posture or appearance. But where do these accessories and costumes used to express individual personality come from? From popular culture, of course, although not necessarily from those images associated with teacher.

Our examination of clothing in popular culture and everyday life supports a conception of identity as a simultaneously social and personal process that involves reconciling, suppressing, ignoring, or dealing in some way with the ambivalence and tensions between different ways of living one's social and personal self under the banner of 'teacher'.

5   Romancing School

Introduction

'School' is still an emotive word in this country; less so than it used to be but still able to raise a degree of nostalgia, interest, love, hatred and antagonisms unlikely, indeed incredible, almost anywhere else. School clings through later life, known and named in reference books, in the briefest biographies, when jobs and appointments are made, and in everyday social life . . . As the subsoil of adult life, . . . 'an invisible compost', school feeds adult feeling of all kinds. (Quigly, 1982, pp. 2–3)

The 'invisible compost' to which Isobel Quigly refers filtered into the British school story of the late nineteenth and early to mid-twentieth century — from Thomas Hughes' book *Tom Brown's School Days* and all of the boys' school stories which followed, to the whole genre of girls' school stories such as those written by Enid Blyton, Elsie Oxenham, Angela Brazil, and Dorita Fairlie Bruce. Like the drawings of teachers that we described in previous chapters, the texts of contemporary children's popular culture carry vestiges of past images situated within the memories and desires of children and adults. This compost of teacher images has a 'romantic' tinge, evoking the sorts of emotions that we associate with the eighteenth and nineteenth century Romantic poets, the 'wishes, fears, love and nostalgia' to which Quigly (1982) refers.

Many of the images of teachers in our collection of drawings were what might be described as romantic hero images, for example, teacher-as-Power-Ranger. Other drawings contain images of romance or desire, for example, teacher-as-fairy princess. Popular culture and drawings are also replete with images of villains — mean, unfair, sexless, lifeless, boring drones who are the anti-heroes of teaching and schooling. We view both sets of images as 'romanticized' because of their inherent hero/anti-hero quality. Following Gerbner's (1963) analysis of teachers in the media, these images could also be described as either larger- or smaller-than-life. In this chapter, we explore the ways in which the images of teacher in children's popular culture can be read as Romantic texts of teaching. We use the word 'romantic' here to refer to upper case 'R' Romance, evoking the conventions of the Romantic movement in poetry and literature. The use of lower case 'r' romance to refer to conventional notions of love, sex, and desire, will be taken up in later chapters.

The educational legacy of the age of Romanticism is insightfully explored by Johann Aitken and other scholars such as John Willinsky, Kieran Egan, Madeleine Grumet, and Jane Roland Martin. As Aitken (1990) notes, the School of Romance at the end of the eighteenth century and beginning of the nineteenth century contained a view of childhood as

> a condition of innocence and our source of hope rather than as a manifestation of original sin or miniature adulthood . . . the child, trailing clouds of glory is an apt symbol of the Romantic ideals of simplicity, innocence, wisdom and an innate harmony with the natural world. (p. 214)

Aitken (1990) observes that 'both Wordsworth and Coleridge congratulate themselves upon having retained something of their childhood selves in their adult lives' (p. 215). Both poets situate the source of their poetic power in their memories of childhood and their desire to return to it. Aitken cites the Hall and Dennis Report, a Canadian curriculum document from the 1960s as the ultimate example of an incurably Romantic view:

> Each [child] and everyone has the right to learn, to play, to laugh, to dream, to love, to dissent, to reach upward, and to be himself. Our children need to be treated as human beings — exquisite, complex, and elegant in their diversity. They must be made to feel that their education heralds the rebirth of an *Age of Wonder* (*ibid*, pp. 215–16).

Such a romanticized notion of the child is taken to its extreme when Hall and Dennis link it to the theme song of *Man of La Mancha*, 'To dream the impossible dream'.

Many popular images can be seen as upper case R Romanticized signposts of Utopia. As film critic Richard Dyer (1985) observes in his analysis of the role of utopianism in children's popular culture:

> [Utopianism is] the image of 'something better' to escape into, or something we want deeply that our day-to-day lives don't provide. Alternatives, hopes, wishes — these are the stuff of utopia, the sense that things could be better, that something other than what is can be imagined and may be realized. (cited in Seiter, 1993, p. 11)

These utopic texts of Teacher in popular culture provide variations on themes such as 'If I ruled the world . . .', or 'if only my teacher were . . .'.

By examining the images from particular movies, books, television shows, ads, and drawings that construct 'teacher', we focus on the ways that certain images persist over time, and the significance of the continuity of these popular culture images to our understanding of the space that teachers occupy in the real and imagined lives of children and their teachers. The challenge is to use the conventions of utopian texts to get underneath the Romanticized larger-than-life/smaller-than-life images of teaching.

A Cultural Reading on the Texts of Teaching

The history of childhood and children's literature is, in a sense, the history of relationships between the adult world and the world of the child based on what Sander Gilman (1985) describes as 'things feared and glorified'. Many of these relationships are lived out in school settings. From Mr. Gradgrind in *David Copperfield* or Ichabod Crane in *The Legend of Sleepy Hollow* to Miss Stacy, in *Anne of Green Gables*, the culture of childhood has been filled with stereotypes and cliches that signal ways in which the adult world generally, and teachers and schools specifically, occupy the fantasy life of children. Many of the texts of popular culture are not separate from each other, but contain particular forms of cross-referencing or what Julia Kristeva describes as an 'intertextual connection' (in Kinder, 1991). For example, a teacher in a popular text might actually be referred to as 'a Miss Grundy-type', a reference to a teacher in the *Archie* comic. Moreover, images in contemporary texts of popular culture often contain images from the texts of another generation. Seiter (1993) provides an excellent example, a television advertisement for 'Sprinkle Chip Ahoy' cookies that was obviously inspired by the 1950s film *Blackboard Jungle*, particularly in its use of rock 'n' roll. While the film was not a musical, it was significant for its 'one o'clock, two o'clock, three o'clock rock' ending, and as Seiter observes: 'In musical commercials the utopian energy of rock-'n'-roll dance stands for the euphoric sugar rush promised by snack foods' (p. 121). The television commercial mimics the 1950s film:

> a bald, bespectacled science teacher drones on with the lesson. A boy removes a bag of cookies from his desk: the instant the teacher turns to the blackboard, the children erupt into wild dancing to a rock beat. They freeze back in their seats when the teacher, totally unaware of what is happening, turns back around. 'Could you explain that again?' the boy asks, so that the party can recommence. (*ibid*)

Although it is likely that the producer of the commercial had seen the film *Blackboard Jungle*, it is highly unlikely that the young viewers (the target audience) would have any idea of the connection. The fact, however, that the ad 'works' successfully for children supports the notion that there are certain conventions in the texts of teaching that are long-lived because they spill over from one generation into the texts of another generation. John Fiske (1987a) describes this textual device as a commodified multigenerational structure:

> The theory of intertextuality proposes that any one text is necessarily read in relationship to others and that a range of textual knowledge

is brought to bear upon it. These relationships do not take the form of specific allusions from one text to another and there is no need for readers to be familiar with specific or the same texts to read inter-textually. Intertextuality exists rather in the space between texts. (cited in Kinder, 1991, p. 45)

As we mentioned in chapter 1, Fiske (1987b) suggests that a cultural study should examine three levels of texts and the relations between these texts. The *primary texts*, which make up the first level of textuality, include the actual episodes of a television series, ad, book, or film, and their relationship to the industry's total production. This notion of relationship to total production is an important one, because a particular series or ad does not stand alone. Madonna, for example, 'is an intertextual conglomerate of television, film, re-cord, radio, posters, etcetera' (*ibid*, p. 285). A close reading of a Disney version of *Beauty and the Beast* is not separate from all the hundreds of versions of *Beauty and the Beast*.

Texts of cultural production are secondary texts. These include the texts that are produced by the culture industry:

studio publicity, television criticism and comment, feature articles about shows and their stars, gossip columns, fan magazines, and so on. They can provide evidence of the ways that the various meanings of the primary text are activated and inserted into the culture for various audiences or subcultures (*ibid*, pp. 285–6).

The third level of textuality, or *reader texts*, refers to the texts that the readers/viewers themselves produce, including:

'their talk about television; their letters to the papers or magazines; their adoption of styles of dress, of speech, or even of thought into their lives'. (*ibid*, pp. 286)

The previous chapters interpret many reader texts, namely the teacher images produced (drawn) or constructed by the children and teachers.

Fiske (*ibid*) argues that because these three levels of textuality 'leak into each other' they demand to be read together if we are to understand the meanings that people make of them. Fiske's (*ibid*) work offers a perspective on cultural texts that moves beyond uncovering the messages contained within popular culture texts:

despite the power of ideology to reproduce itself in its subjects, de-spite the hegemonic force of the dominant classes, the people still manage to make their own meanings and to construct their own cul-ture within, and often against, that which the industry provides for them. Cultural studies aims to understand and encourage this cultural democracy at work. (p. 286)

We nonetheless heed the cautionary note of Farber, Provenzo, and Holm (1994) who observe that 'it is possible to romanticize the open capacity of readers to invent fresh meanings for texts and create their own culture' (p. 11). This same position is taken up by Jane Miller (1990) who refers to 'a sanctioned liberality of readings, which leaves meaning and pleasure and value to individual readers spinning in eccentric isolation' (p. 158). Our work in the previous chapters on image and metaphor supports the notion that there is no one simple interpretation of how particular images and metaphors contribute to the professional identity of teachers, or on how cultural images of teachers are constructed.

Alison Lurie (1990) suggests that the non-canonized texts of children's popular culture,' because they often lack the subtleties and nuances of more sophisticated texts, become ideal texts for pushing cliches and stereotypes to the surface. In this regard, they are like the drawings that we analyzed in the previous chapters. Lurie (1990) credits the appeal of non-canonized children's texts to the fact that their authors seem to remember what it is like to be a child. In referring to non-canonized texts, she includes all those texts that are not regarded as 'good' children's literature: most serial fiction, most television shows, and the Disney texts in all of their manifestations (print, television shows, movies, lunchkits). Included in this list would be the texts to which we have already referred and to which we shall return later in the chapter: the *Sweet Valley* series, *My Little Pony Tales, Boy Meets World,* and the *Nancy Drew Mystery* series.

In the sections that follow, we consider the invisible compost of teachers and schooling in the culture of childhood in two ways: (i) through an examination of the texts of cultural production, we consider how popular culture becomes a vehicle for circulating a code of Romanticism; (ii) through close readings of several primary texts from popular culture, we show how such texts reveal widely used conventions of teaching. By making explicit the ways in which each of these texts draws on and leaks into other popular culture texts of teaching, we investigate the script for a cumulative cultural text.

The Texts of Cultural Production

Texts of cultural production 'provide evidence of the ways that the various meanings of the primary text are activated and inserted into the culture for various audiences or subcultures' (Fiske, 1987b, pp. 285–6). Authors' and critics' views of the primary texts of children's popular culture provide important insights and contexts for interpreting their impact and imagery. For example, a close reading of Lurie (1990) suggests that in a sense, she romanticizes the notion of the children's author off in a corner, away from other adults, pouring out personal memories of real childhood. She ignores the fact that many of the non-canonized texts of which she speaks are churned out as part of an editorial factory. Episodes of series fiction such as *Sweet Valley High, Nancy Drew* or the *Hardy Boys*, for example, are written by many different ghostwriters. Moreover, even ghostwriters have a limited hand in the writing since there is also an editorial team which monitors the details of each episode to ensure that texts are consistent (Mitchell and Reid-Walsh, in press). Lurie (1990) also makes reference to the significance of memory and forgetting in rather sweeping ways, whereas such constructs demand, instead, to be problematized (Haug, 1987; Sutherland, 1992; Weiler, 1992).

At the same time, however, Lurie (1990) is right about two things: non-canonized popular culture texts are by definition popular, which implies that they manage to tap into the particular desires of the child reader. Moreover, non-canonized texts are, for the most part, unmediated by adults beyond the writers and production team. In other words, since adults often dismiss non-canonized texts as by definition not worthy of attention, these texts become what Lurie calls the 'sacred' texts of childhood because they represent an exclusionary world to which only the child usually has access. Teachers and librarians frequently refuse to stock such texts, and rarely admit them into the discourse of the classroom. Yet, non-canonized texts provide a window onto what children really like, and should thus be of great interest to educators.

What enables some adults to write a successful popular text for children? The secret might lie partly in the ability to remember what it is like to be a child, and partly in the fact that many aspects of childhood desire and fantasy transcend generations through the medium of culture. As Kim Reynolds (1990) observes:

> Today's juvenile fiction carries within it images, structures, attitudes and value systems which are at least partially shaped by their earlier counterparts. One obvious reason for this relationship is that the adult writers of contemporary fiction were once child readers of fiction written for them and so are in some ways responding to what they experienced. (p. 152)

The response of adults to what they themselves experienced as children is sometimes an abiding sympathy with childhood dilemmas that leads to adult-generated counter-texts for children. The significance of text-counter-text in the memory of adult writers is an important one. As Seiter (1993) observes:

> A separate children's playground and street culture has existed as long as children have lived in cities and gone to school: but this was a culture produced by children and passed from child to child. A similar kind of culture is now produced by adults and offered to children through the mass media from toddlerhood onward. Advertising agencies have borrowed the themes of children's culture and redefined them with a focus on consumer culture. In James's formulation, 'Adult order is manipulated so that what adults esteem is made to appear

ridiculous; what adults despise is invested with prestige.' Adults are often the butt of television commercials' jokes. Thus commercials invite children at an early age to identify with other children (some of them peers, some of them older) rather than with their parents. Teachers and parents are subjected to various forms of rebellion or humiliation. (p. 117)

Francine Pascal, the author of the Sweet Valley Series, is one of the most successful at tapping into what children like by writing what she describes as a counter-text to her own childhood experience. As we noted in chapter 1, the series is marketed exclusively for girls, has spawned several other series targeted at different age groups, and is probably the best selling popular series in the world. Throughout the entire series, teachers and school provide the backdrop for episodes in the lives of the Wakefield twins. Why would an author use school to such an extent in her books? Pascal answers this question in a secondary text by discussing her personal images of school:

I absolutely hated high school. Learning by rote made the whole system repressive. The 'Sweet Valley High' series draws a lot on my own high school experiences. Going to high school in the fifties, as I did, was not appreciably different from going to high school in the eighties . . . All of us think high school is wonderful for everyone else. The 'Sweet Valley High' series come out of what I fantasized high school was like for everyone but me. (Garrett and McCue, 1989, p. 194)

What is interesting here is not so much that school was a negative experience for Pascal, but rather that she has crafted a series where school is written as the counter-text to her own everyday experiences of schooling. Thomas Hughes, the author of *Tom Brown's Schooldays*, on the other hand, has a different perspective on his own writing. In a preface to the sixth edition of the book, he notes that he wrote the book on the occasion of his son going off to boarding school:

Why, my whole object in writing at all was to get the chance of preaching! When a man comes into my time of life and has his bread to make, and very little time to spare, is it likely that he will spend almost the whole of his yearly vacation in writing a story just to amuse people? I think not. At any rate, I wouldn't do so myself . . . My sole object in writing was to preach to boys: if ever I write again, it will be to preach to some other age. I can't see that a man has any business to write at all unless he has something which he thoroughly believes and wants to preach about. If he has this, and the chance of delivering himself of it, let him by all means put it in the shape in which it is most likely to get a hearing; but let him never be so carried away as to forget that preaching is his object. (cited in Quigly, 1982, p. 42)

While they do at least signal the possibilities of constructing what might be described as texts and counter-texts (or what Frigga Haug, 1987), describes as working against the text), these secondary texts of cultural production are, in a sense, 'prepared statements'. Like any text, they are problematized by questions of memory and intention. How frankly do authors remember or reveal their intentions? For example, Angela Brazil, author of many of the girls' school stories in the 1920s–40s presents herself and the intentions behind her school stories in a relatively unproblematized way:

> To be able to write for young people depends, I consider, largely upon whether you are able to retain your early attitude of mind while acquiring a certain facility with your pen. It is a mistake ever to grow up! I confess I am still an absolute schoolgirl in my sympathies. (cited in Freeman, 1976, p. 18)

Over the years, however, she has received a great deal of attention with regard to intention from a number of critics such as Musgrave, Freeman, Quigly and Auchmuty who have speculated that actually, her school girl stories were intentionally encoded lesbian texts.

In the section which follows, we move from these secondary texts of author intentionality to the presence of 'nostalgia, interest, love, hatred and antagonism' (Quigly, 1982, p. 1) in the primary texts of schooling in contemporary popular culture.

The Primary Texts

Barnyard Battle: Sweet Valley High

What if suddenly you had a teacher who was beautiful and did interesting things in school — like going out on field trips?

We began chapter 1 with an excerpt from *Barnyard Battle*, an episode in the *Sweet Valley* fiction series. In this episode Jessica and Elizabeth Wakefield are introduced to a student teacher, Ms. Shepard, the embodiment of every student's dream. Not only does Ms. Shepard walk into class on the first day of school dressed, as we noted in chapter 1, in a way that totally ruptures the children's expectations, but she also promptly announces a change in curriculum:

> I'll begin by telling you what we'll be studying for the next few weeks. Jessica sighed. Mrs. Arnette had already told the class they would be learning about American pioneers — again. It seemed to Jessica that every social studies class she had ever been in had had a unit on pioneers. Not even a cool, young teacher could make that topic interesting. (Suzanne, 1992, p. 5)

Jessica immediately adopts a 'school is boring' attitude:

> 'Social studies is an exciting topic', Ms. Shepard began cheerfully. 'Social studies is a boring subject', Jessica corrected mentally. (*ibid*)

Following the groans of the class, Ms. Shepard with a wry smile observes:

> I'm glad to see you're familiar with the subject . . . But perhaps you aren't familiar with the way I'm going to teach it. First of all, we won't be using any textbooks. Nothing I teach you about pioneers will come out of a book . . . She opened up a folder, pulled out a photograph, and began to walk up and down the aisles with it.
> I think the best way for you to learn is for me to *show* you pioneer life, not tell you about it. (*ibid*, p. 6)

Here we see a so-called subversion of conventional teaching practice that appears in many popular culture texts: Not only does Ms. Shepard propose to dispense with the prescribed pedagogy, she introduces a counter curriculum that wins the admiration of her students. We learn of this from a discussion in which her students are engaged after class at Casey's Place, the local hang-out:

> 'I have a bad case of biology blues', she (Janet) said with a sigh.
> 'I know what you mean', Mary Wallace said sympathetically. 'I'll probably have to stay up until midnight to get all my homework done.'
> 'Teachers are inhuman', Janet said.
> 'Not all teachers', Mandy remarked, 'Ms. Shepard's great.'
> 'Who's Ms. Shepard?', Janet asked.
> 'I can't believe you haven't heard about her', Jessica said. 'Everybody at school is talking about her. She's a student-teacher in our social studies class. She's young, and really pretty. Her class is awesome.'
> 'She showed us how to use berries and plants for make-up', Ellen Riteman added, sipping her ice water.
> 'A teacher talked about makeup?' Janet asked, beginning to look interested. 'During class?' . . .
> Janet rolled her eyes. 'This is embarrassing. We're sitting here talking about school.' She glanced around the restaurant. 'I hope nobody overheard us.' (*ibid*, pp. 12–13)

Eventually we learn what Ms. Shepard has in mind in terms of 'showing' rather than 'telling':

> Since we're studying pioneers, we're going to experience pioneer life firsthand. There's an authentic working pioneer farm over in Corona Valley . . . All of Mrs. Arnette's classes are going to get to spend a weekend there, and you're the first! (*ibid*, p. 25)

Naturally all of this outdoor education is too much for the regular teachers who only go along to supervise.

> 'She (Mrs Arnette) looks a little tired', Elizabeth said.
> Caroline nodded, 'And have you ever seen her hair so messy? It looks like a little kid did her bun this morning.'
> 'Look at the way she's rubbing her eyes.' Julie noted. 'She keeps talking about coffee . . .'
> 'Maybe you should have made a bet with the teachers instead of with the boys, Elizabeth', Julie said with a smile. 'It's the teachers who seem to be falling apart!'
> 'Teachers just don't have the stuff pioneers are made of', Caroline declared. (*ibid*, p. 95)

In these excerpts we see that Ms. Shepard, by freeing her students from the confinement of the classroom and books, romances natural learning, nature, and the significance of personal experience. We also see her rupture the notion that the world of children and adults don't mix. Unlike the regular teachers in the school, she is accepted into the world of Elizabeth, Jessica, and their friends.

An Apple for Starlight: My Little Pony Tales

> What if your regular teacher suddenly got sick and you had to take over the class? . . .

My Little Pony Tales, a half-hour television cartoon show, is based on the My Little Pony figures developed by Hasbro in the late 1970s. The market for My Little Pony figures and accessories, as well as the cartoon series, is primarily girls between the ages of 3 and 7. Each half-hour segment includes episodes that regularly involve the actions of the little ponies who occupy Ponyland: Starlight, Bonbon, Patch, Ace, Teddy, Lancer, Melody, Bright Eyes, and Sweetheart. While it is important to point out that not all episodes of *My Little Pony Tales* are centred on schooling, many are. For example, in the episode entitled 'An Apple for Starlight', the pony-teacher, Miss Hackney suddenly takes ill in the middle of her science lesson on pulleys. She calls upon one of the female pony students, Starlight to take over the class. When Starlight takes over, chaos reigns with paper airplanes flying every which way. She elicits the help of two of her friends who join in a singing routine that is supposed to motivate the others to want to learn instead of fooling around.

> Reading, writing, doesn't always seem exciting, still next time you get depressed when cramming for tomorrow's test: stop delaying, though you'd rather be out playing, give your thoughts to study for a spell.

When the song and dance approach doesn't help to settle the class, Starlight goes to the washroom where she faces herself in the mirror and reflects on why she is being unsuccessful. She concludes that, rather than emulate Miss Hackney; she must just be herself. We see here a version of 'to thine own self be true', a theme that often occurs as a type of divine intervention or sudden insight. Starlight thus returns to the classroom with new insights about herself and succeeds in engaging the class with an active experienced-based pedagogy when she takes the whole class on a field trip.

While the focus of her field trip was to be history, the lesson returns to the scientific principle behind pulleys when Starlight and the class find themselves stranded in some caves. By seizing on these scientific principles, Starlight saves the day. As in *Barnyard Battle*, we see that the success of the lesson is related to the significance of outdoor education and hands-on experience, 'proving' once again that in-class learning is not only boring, but also irrelevant and a waste of time. Ultimately, Miss Hackney returns to the classroom, pleased that all has gone well and gives an apple to Starlight, the substitute teacher.

What kinds of images of teaching and teachers are portrayed in this episode? Although Miss Hackney, a pair of glasses falling down over her nose, is presented as stern, she cannot keep the class in order. We are not sure whether this is just an off-day for Miss Hackney, or whether she really has difficulty with discipline. We do, however, find out that several students habitually misbehave. For example, Melody is always hooked up to her walkman and Bonbon is always eating in class. The lyrics to Starlight's song and dance routine confirm the stereotype that teachers regularly make school work boring.

We also see in this episode a romantic version of 'natural teaching'. Starlight has no formal teacher preparation; indeed she is a student herself. In the end her natural teaching evokes superhero powers since she is able to rescue her charges from being trapped in a cave. Thus, not only is school deinstitutionalized (with most of the main action taking place on a school trip), but the work of teachers is also heroized, since schools are so boring, dreadful, so irrelevant and the learning so meaningless that only some superhero heroic deed can save the day.

Prime Time Teachers: 'Boy Meets World'

What if your teacher suddenly said, 'Okay, you teach the class . . .'

Boy Meets World, an American television sit-com that began in 1993, regularly features Cory 'the boy' and the domestic episodes in his life that just happen to include living next door to his sixth grade teacher, Mr. Feeny, a middle-aged, very respectable British gentleman. Much of the show's intended humour centres around Cory's 'typical boy' disinterest in school and all things academic, and Mr. Feeny's 'typical teacher' daily task of trying to inculcate

knowledge and values into Cory — both at home and at school. In one episode, we encounter another version of Starlight's 'if I could be teacher for the
day . . .' The episode begins with Cory's observation to his friends:

> It's not very hard to teach sixth grade . . . you know, same stuff every
> year. The only thing that changes is the students . . . The teacher doesn't
> really do anything, you read the book, you pass the test.

Mr. Feeny decides to take Cory up on his challenge that anyone can
teach, turning the social studies class over to Cory for the week. At the end of
the unit, the class will be tested. If the students do as well or better on the test
after Cory's teaching, Mr. Feeny will pay Cory a fifth of his salary. If the
students do not do as well as they would have normally been expected to do,
Cory will give Mr. Feeny his new bike. The topic that Cory is to teach is
prejudice and the teaching tool is to be the novel *The Diary of Anne Frank*.

Cory is very sure that this is going to be a snap bet. He comes into school
on the first day of his tenure as the cool teacher dressed as one of the students,
and asks to be called 'Hey Dude'. Mr. Feeny, no longer the teacher, too dresses
casually, wearing a baseball hat and shirt. So convinced is Cory that teachers
have nothing to do but assign work, that he decides he is not even going to
bother reading the novel although he assigns it to the students to read. Eventually of course, all hell breaks loose — no-one is listening to him or learning
anything. Even the class genius is sloughing off. Mr. Feeny joins in with the
rest of the class in their mutinous 'we're not going to do anything' behaviour
and learns to play poker with Sean, another student. Cory begins to accept the
fact that he really isn't going to be able to deliver on the boast since he is not
succeeding in getting the students to learn: 'I'm a crummy teacher and I resign.'

While in this case the fault lies clearly with the 'teacher' we see here
another version of the desperate 'I'm not reaching the students' scene that
teachers like Starlight encounter.

It is time for a divine intervention and a sudden insight experience. It
comes when Cory sees his older brother's girlfriend in tears following a racist
comment that was made to her. She is an Asian American who has been
harassed for her Asian heritage. Cory is so outraged not only at the injustice
of it, but also at the fact that this could still happen. He is moved to see
parallels between the life of the girlfriend and the life of Anne Frank. He goes
into class the next day dressed-to-teach in a jacket, dress shirt and tie — in
contrast to his peers in the class who call him Mr. GQ (from *Gentlemen's
Quarterly* magazine). Cory is ready to talk to his classmates 'about prejudice
and how it exists in today's world'. He drives his point home by asking about
the non-American heritage of a student in the class and by calling him a 'wop'.
The demonstration about injustice is such an inspiring one that his peers have
no alternative but to learn. Naturally they do as well on the test as they would
have with Mr. Feeny. One student who normally does very poorly does particularly well. Once again, the classroom has become a dramatic scene with

the teacher stand-in conquering the ignorance of the students through the pedagogy of personal experience.

Where the Curriculum is Murder: The Nancy Drew Mystery Series

What if 'on the surface' you were sitting through a boring droning history lesson, but deep down you were really solving a murder mystery . . . ?

We are interested in hero series texts such as *Nancy Drew*, and the *The Hardy Boys*, where teachers have been conspicuous by their absence in order to show that when they do appear, it is as anti-hero texts within the code of upper case R Romance. This is particularly the case in *Nancy Drew*, an American series for girls initiated by Edward Stratemeyer in 1930. The 18-year-old sleuth, Nancy Drew, already has a larger-than-lifeness about her: she lives with her widowed father, Carson Drew the lawyer, who gives her a great deal of responsibility, frequently bringing her in on his cases. In charge of the management of their house, Nancy oversees the work of their housekeeper, Hannah Gruen. The very fact that Nancy has her own car, can outperform almost all adults, and is independent and autonomous is part of her long-lasting appeal to her readership of girls between the ages of 9 and 12 (Caprio, 1992; Deane, 1991; Mason, 1975; Reid-Walsh and Mitchell, 1993).

Throughout the Nancy Drew Mystery Series, there are few references to school or authority in general. Because Nancy, who has been 18-years-old for most of the sixty-three years of her existence, is slightly beyond school age. She is normally portrayed outside the bounds and controls of school. A book where Nancy spends time in school thus stands out, and yields important insights about teachers. In #1 of the Nancy Drew Files, *Secrets Can Kill*, Nancy is called into Bedford High as an undercover detective to solve a case of a series of thefts. As the promotional blurb on the book jacket describes it, 'Nancy Drew goes back to high school — but this time, the curriculum is murder.' From the time of her arrival at the school we become aware of the smaller-than-lifeness of Mr. Parton, the school principal:

Stepping into the office, Nancy took one look at Mr. Parton and decided to try to solve this case in record time. Not only did she want that weekend with Ned, but Mr. Parton looked like he was on the verge of a nervous breakdown. For the sake of his health she'd better work fast!

'It's driving me insane!' Mr. Parton declared, dramatically pounding his fists against his temples. 'And are the police any help? Noooo. Beef up security, they say. Ha! . . . Thank heavens I know your father.

If he hadn't suggested that I hire you, I don't know what I'd have done.'

'Probably collapse', Nancy told herself, but she kept her thoughts silent. (Keene, 1986, pp. 15–16)

Because she is an undercover agent disguised as a transfer student, Nancy as a 'substitute student' must fit into the classes. The reader is thus offered glimpses of her views of teachers and school learning:

Nancy's next class was American history. She'd almost forgotten just how boring a bad teacher could be, but the droning voice, the intimi-dating looks, all of it reminded her why she'd been happy to leave high school behind. She'd certainly be happy to leave history behind! The forty-five minute period dragged on and on. Halfway through, Nancy let her mind wander. Anything was better than the teacher's monotone. When American history was finally over, Nancy heaved a sigh of relief along with the rest of the students.

'Class', the teacher called over the noise of the final bell, 'read the next two chapters in your textbook for homework'.

'Great', Nancy groaned to herself. 'Boring homework, too.' The Bedford High mystery was turning out to have hidden liabilities! (*ibid*, pp. 25–6).

Nancy's teachers fit the stereotype of most of the other adults who regularly feature in this series. Adults and their institutions, such as schools and the law, are always secondary to the amateur detecting feats of Nancy. Thus, teachers are part of a class of adults such as the police, who cannot be expected to know what is going on. Of course, amidst all of this droning and groaning on the part of teachers, fretting on the part of the principal and the usual inept-ness on the part of the police, Nancy manages to solve both the case of the thefts of school property, as well as the murder of the star school athlete.

Reading the Signs: Codes and Conventions

At the beginning of this chapter we conjectured that one of the ways in which the invisible compost of schooling feeds into the fantasy life of children and adults is through the larger-than-life/smaller-than-life images of teachers con-tained in the popular culture of childhood. In this section, we look at how the code of upper case R Romance in teaching saturates many of the texts of the popular culture of childhood through particular conventions of teaching that recur. We use a semiotic notion of codes and conventions to provide a useful framework for considering the intertextuality of teachers in films (both intergenerationally as well as across contemporary texts) and to provide a lens on the cumulative cultural text of teaching. Of particular significance to our analysis is the way these conventions 'saturate' the dominant ideology of teaching, locating the literature on the professional identity of teachers within the prior social knowledge that Roland Barthes describes as 'historical, cultural, and institutional' (cited in Allen, 1987, p. 5).

Angela McRobbie's work on magazines for teenage girls identifies ways in which the dominant ideology of femininity saturates the lives of young women through particular codes and conventions contained within these magazines . . . She maps out a framework for a cultural reading of these codes of femininity using a semiotic analysis. Drawing on the work of Barthes, McRobbie (1991) observes that

> a semiological analysis proceeds by isolating sets of codes around which the message is constructed . . . These codes constitute the 'rules' by which different meanings are produced and it is the identification and consideration of these in detail that provides the basis to the analysis. (pp. 91–92)

A code, she observes contains both a literal or denotative level, and a connotative level which depends on 'prior social knowledge on the part of the reader, observer or audience' (*ibid*, p. 93). One such code, the code of romance, for example, is supported by certain conventions or recurring themes such as 'the convention of extending luck or coincidence by the introduction of supernatural devices' (*ibid*, p. 96).

On one hand, the codes and conventions that we identify in the texts of teaching might be read simply as the conventions of Hollywood. As Todd Gitlin observes, 'Hollywood movies have largely been blind to the workings of institutions. Where they excel is with villains' (cited in Farber *et al.*, 1994, p. 168). Hollywood teacher texts provide all the ingredients of fantasy: heroes and anti-heroes, good and evil, child or protagonist as omnipotent, freedom from entrapment. In short, they offer a version of 'if I ruled the world'. On the other hand, writers and producers, having chosen to situate their comedy, drama, ad, action hero or romance text in school, draw upon particular episodes and recurring themes that are 'out there' in the general culture.

In the previous section we looked at the raw material, the denotative level of teacher texts. In the section that follows we consider the connotative level in which we identify codes and conventions of upper case R Romance: 'if I were sitting in the teacher's desk. . . .' These conventions exist in both adult texts as well as the texts of childhood. While not all fictionalized accounts of teaching contain all of these conventions, we think that they are frequent enough to be considered more than just accidental. In order to demonstrate the leakage of these conventions from one text into another, we include in our analysis the four texts from the previous section, as well as the well-known Hollywood teacher texts *Teachers, To Sir With Love, Blackboard Jungle, Dead Poets Society, Kindergarten Cop*, and *Stand and Deliver.*

Codes and Conventions of Upper Case R Romance in the Texts of Teaching

Teacher as outsider

Much of the dramatic significance in these teacher texts of popular culture is based on a contrast between smaller-than-life *real* teachers and larger-than-life *stand-in* teachers. It is the stand-in teachers who perform 'superhero' teaching feats. We saw an example of this in *Barnyard Battle* where Ms. Shepard is the student teacher. Starlight and Cory are examples of children who stand in for the regular teacher. As well, the cumulative cultural text of Nancy Drew is such that she always knows more than adults in real positions of authority — including the police and teachers. Other larger-than-life stand-in teachers include John Kimble from the film *Kindergarten Cop*; Mr. Thackeray, in *To Sir With Love* who is an engineer-turned teacher in his first teaching assignment; Mr. Dadier in *Blackboard Jungle*, also on his first teaching assignment; and Mr. Escalante, in *Stand and Deliver*, a computer-expert who becomes a stand-in mathematics teacher since the school he is assigned to has no computers. In the movie *Teachers*, one of the most successful teachers is a patient who escapes from a psychiatric ward of a nearby hospital!

Farber *et al.* (1994) focus on the outsider role of Hollywood teachers in their consideration of teachers-as-hero texts, noting that the otherness of characters like Mr. Escalante offers rich possibilities for multiple and even conflicting perspectives.

> We encounter characters who quickly fall into either the camp of the near and good or that of the enemy (or irrelevant). The outsider figure of the educator-hero often seems peculiar, but only in ways that prove him (or her) to be worthy of the students' respect . . . we deal almost exclusively with characters who seem vary familiar, and whose potential otherness — the possibility of genuinely conflicting views among reasonable and sympathetically presented characters — we never experience in these tales. (p. 169)

Teaching is natural

It is also a convention of these texts that formal teacher preparation is mostly unnecessary — so that teaching is regarded as a natural act. This contributes to an ideology of 'born teachers', and contrasts with popular culture images of other professionals such as doctors whose training is often the dramatic focus (for example, films such as *The Interns*, and television shows such as *Ben Casey, Saint Elsewhere*, and *ER*).

Thus, as we have seen, Cory, Starlight, and John Kimble become teachers because of circumstances. Others, such as Mr. Thackeray and Mr. Escalante have clearly not become teachers as a first choice of a career. Moreover, novice teachers such as Kimble, Thackeray, and Escalante contrast positively with the 'burned out/bummed out' experienced teachers whom we meet in the conventional staffroom scenes. Ms. Shepard and Mr. Dadier are two of the few teachers who have received professional training, Ms. Shepard as an education major from nearby Sweet Valley College, and Mr. Dadier as a student teacher on the GI Bill. However, as we learn in the book *Blackboard Jungle*, Mr. Dadier learned nothing about real classrooms during his professional training.

The 'ordinary' in school is irrelevant (Farber et al., 1994, p. 171)

As Farber *et al.* observe, in the majority of Hollywood teacher films, what happens in schools is not worth noticing. The irrelevancy of the ordinary becomes conventionalized in a number of ways:

Making a dramatic entrance
This is accomplished through a variety of conventionalized film and narrative techniques. Through dress and/or gestures idealized teachers often enter the classroom in such a way that they are immediately set off from regular teachers. This can be seen in Starlight's song and dancing routine, Ms. Shepard's dress and appearance (see opening quote of chapter 1), and Cory's dress and demeanour (when he enters the classroom to really teach, he is no longer wearing his 'cool dude' outfit but rather his 'GQ' attire). The technique of using long camera shots that follow the protagonist into the classroom highlights the dramatic entrance. For example, we follow Miss Brodie's path of cycling from her home to the school, and later, through the lingering gazes of the art teacher and the music teacher, right into the classroom. A similar extended film segment at the beginning of *Stand and Deliver* follows Mr. Escalante's modest car into the Hispanic neighbourhood and leads up to his opening dramatic act in the classroom. Similarly, the camera follows Mr. Thackeray in *To Sir With Love* through the neighbourhood, into the schoolyard, and down the hallway of the school to his classroom. As well, in *Kindergarten Cop* we follow Mr. Kimble along the road and to the school through long camera shots. The accompanying sound tracks in these films frequently contribute to the dramatic and romanticized entrance.

Liberating students from the usual school curriculum
We refer here to the ways in which certain 'romanticized' teachers in popular culture distinguish themselves from ordinary classroom teachers through innovative pedagogy and curriculum. Examples include Ms. Shepard's announcement that the unit on pioneers would involve a field trip instead of boring books, Starlight's taking the class out on a field trip, and Cory's signalling of a free-for-all. These exceptional teachers win over their students by providing a sharp contrast to the dull droning classes that Nancy Drew must sit through, the sort one normally expects in a world dominated by dull 'unromanticized'

adults. Additional dramatic examples can be found in Mr. Thackeray's gestures of throwing textbooks in the waste basket in *To Sir With Love*, Mr. Keating's tearing out pages from the poetry text in *Dead Poets Society*; Mr. Dadier's media class where he finally 'gets through' to his students; and Miss Brodie's lecture on a romanticized, personal version of history, where she dramatically replaces the hanging portrait of Prime Minister Stanley Baldwin with a painting by Giotto. Miss Brodie, also romanticizes the notion of 'natural learning' through field trips to museums, art galleries, art studios, or simply sitting outdoors under a tree rather than in a classroom. Each of these scenes builds on a Romantic notion of freedom and escape from the dull dreary classroom.

Teaching as sudden enlightenment, divine intervention, or the 'aha' experience
Consistent with the notion that teachers do not need professional training is the recognition that real teaching is often guided by sudden insight. This we see in Starlight's sudden recognition that she must simply be herself, and Cory's sudden 'aha' experience where he connects the racial harassment of his brother's girlfriend to the life of Anne Frank. This sudden enlightenment can also be found in scenes like Mr. Thackeray's sudden awareness that he must treat the students like adults, Mr. Escalante's sudden insights on how to teach his students by coming to class dressed as a chef, or using an apple to teach fractions. Mr. Dadier, too, has radical insights about 'getting through' to his delinquents by making his lessons relevant to their lives.

Scenes with regular anti-hero teachers
The romanticized stand-in teachers are frequently presented as oppositional texts in scenes with the regular teachers. For example, we see Miss Hackney as ordinary through the action of Starlight who saves the day; the American history teacher as boring through the hero text of Nancy who always knows better than adults; and Mrs. 'Hairnet' Arnette as strict and humourless in contrast with the beautiful, young, well-dressed imaginative 'with it' teacher, Ms. Shepard. The convention in adult teacher films such as *Teachers, To Sir With Love, Blackboard Jungle, and Stand and Deliver* is to include some form of staffroom scene in order to spotlight the heroic sterling qualities of the protagonist against the backdrop of drab, lifeless men and dowdy, bossy matrons who seem to constitute most of the regular staff.

Final conquering scene
Most of these popular culture texts have some final heroizing event as a result of the actions of the stand-in heroized teacher. For example, Starlight manages to rescue all the ponies in her charge by her clever application of the 'boring' knowledge about pulleys and history to an escape from a cave. Cory is so successful in his 'aha' insight about the relevance of Anne Frank that the students all do well on the unit test. These conquering scenes can be seen in the student achievement of Mr. Escalante's mathematics class and in the successes of juvenile delinquent/hoodlum students of Mr. Dadier and Mr.

Thackeray. As the teacher-activist Alex Jurrell (Nick Nolte) in the movie *Teachers* proclaims to one of his colleagues: 'The damn school wasn't built for us, Roger. It wasn't built for your unions, your lawyers, all your other institutions. It was built for the kids. And they're here for us. We're here for them. That's what it's all about — kids.' Farber *et al.* (1994) remark that:

> when all is said and done, we walk away with the sense of finished business. The game has been won, the school has been saved, the test has been passed, the villains once encountered are history, sometimes slinking off in ignominy, as in *Lean on Me*, or left on scene looking ridiculous and small as in *Dead Poets Society*. Problems overcome in triumph dissolve before our eyes . . . (p. 168)

Thus, teaching is presented as a dramatic episode — and once the conquering has taken place, either in terms of the students or administration, then there is the possibility of a 'happily ever after' existence.

Teaching is a heroic and solitary act

The romanticization of the individual 'hero' text can be seen in the classrooms of Starlight, Cory, and Ms. Shepard. Generally, the other teachers in the school, are portrayed as 'anti-heroes' and villains: Miss Hackey because she can't 'hack it', Mr. Feeny because 'he just teaches the same thing year after year: and Mrs. 'Hairnet' Arnette along with the other teachers who can't even last on the pioneer village expedition. This can also be seen in texts such as *Stand and Deliver* where only Mr. Escalante can see that he could be doing more to ensure that the students learn. In *To Sir With Love*, it is only Mr. Thackeray who stands out against a backdrop of teachers who have given up, and in *Blackboard Jungle*, Mr. Dadier is the one with the burning desire to 'get through' to the students. Farber, *et al.* (1994) note that this 'special hero' solitary hero status is of dubious value beyond a general uplifting of spirits:

> For while the message is conveyed that transformative action is pos-sible, that action seems always to be a product of special heroes, working alone — often even entering from outside and never fitting in. Transformation is always a product of masculine charisma and unique interpersonal relationships . . . Nor is there any suggestion of shared work among adults of good will to achieve any transformative ends together. Escalante walks off alone into the sunset. Other good teachers might emulate his efforts and transform the prospects of some other group of deserving kids, but the focus and method of change is always personal, the private dealings of a bunch of good people who find themselves happily together, cut off from and superior to a world whose workings they must largely accept. (p. 171)

From Print to Screen: Intertext

By comparing visual and print versions of the same text, it is possible to 'read over the shoulders' of the script writers to see how certain scenes or images of teaching become 'conventionalized' and romanticized for a mass-market audience. For example, the novel *Anne of Green Gables*, widely read around the world by generations of students, has been variously re-scripted for television and for the stage, including a musical script and score adaptation written by Norman Campbell and Mavor Moore. These varying formats all feature Anne's beloved teacher Miss Stacy, and provide an ideal site for investigating the notion of 'conventionalizing' heroic qualities of teachers. Clearly the work of transforming a 329-page novel into a musical production for the stage, for example, necessitates a great deal of poetic licence. Many scenes must be left out, and the scriptwriter must choose scenes which will not only 'carry the story' in a condensed form, but also maintain the integrity of the author, and at the same time evoke a particular artistic response.

In the novel *Anne of Green Gables* we first meet Miss Stacy through a second-hand account where Anne is telling her guardian Marilla about Miss Stacy based on what she heard from the other girls in the class:

> The girls all think she is perfectly sweet. Diana says she has the love-
> liest fair curly hair and such fascinating eyes. She dresses beautifully,
> and her sleeve puffs are much bigger than anybody else's in Avonlea
> ... And the Friday afternoons they don't have recitations Miss Stacy
> takes them all to the woods for a 'field' day and they study ferns and
> flowers and birds. And they have physical culture exercises every
> morning and evening. Mrs. Lynde says she never heard of such goings-
> on and it all comes of having a lady teacher. But I think it must be
> splendid and I believe I shall find that Miss Stacy is a kindred spirit.
> (Montgomery, 1909/1942, p. 189)

While the references to Miss Stacy at the beginning of chapter 24 of a 36-chapter book is rather brief, Campbell and Moore capture something of the significance of this liberating 'kindred spirit' who enters Anne's imaginative life — particularly through the lyrics to the song that she sings. The words have a conventional liberating romantic quality in opposition to 'book learning', based on naturalness and the belief that knowledge and goodness are contained within the child:

> Open the window!
> Sweep out the cobwebs
> Open your mind to what is going all around
> Look at the sunlight
> What is it made of?
> How can it make the flowers

jump right out of the ground?
Open your ears
Use that old nose
How come a queen bee knows a rose?
Take off the blinkers!
Let in the daylight!
Why does the clinging ivy cling?
Tear down the fences!
Use those five senses!
Learn everything!
(Lyrics: Norman Campbell; music: Mavor Moore, 1969)

Multi-versioned texts such as the novel *Blackboard Jungle* by Evan Hunter and the 1953 film version starring Glenn Ford offer similar points of entry for considering the ways in which popular culture contributes to a particular construction of narrative accounts of teaching. The novel *The Prime of Miss Jean Brodie* written by Muriel Spark (1961) and the film version starring Maggie Smith has evoked extensive literary criticism that sheds light on the codes and conventions of teaching. For example, Mary Cadogan and Patricia Craig (1986) offer a reading of the novel *The Prime of Miss Jean Brodie* that takes into account the texts of schooling that Muriel Spark read as a child. One series of texts, they argue, particularly certain school stories by Dorita Fairlie Bruce, 'leak into' the adult school story of *The Prime of Miss Jean Brodie*. As Cadogan and Craig (1986) observe, Fairlie Bruce's writing included

'prefect-worship, midnight gambollings, empty-headed gossip, a pre-occupation with aids to beauty — everything, in fact, but an interest in sex in its smuttier aspects, with which all 11- and 12-year-olds are obsessed'. (p. 183)

They contend that the reason why Spark writes *The Prime of Miss Jean Brodie* in the voice of the 11- and 12-year-old girls is so that she could capture directly the preoccupations of girls of this age — including their preoccupation with sex. As Cadogan and Craig (1986) observe:

all of the unmentionable — or at least unacknowledged — elements of school life which the children's author (Bruce) had no means of suggesting are composed, in the adult view, into a reconstruction which integrates childhood experiences and their later significance. This is true to a certain extent of all comparisons of school stories written for children with those written for adults, but in a particular way it is true here: the stringent exactness which Muriel Spark has brought to her view of real-life schoolgirls is paralleled by the exact-ness of Dorita Fairlie Bruce's assessment of their fantasy counterparts. (p. 183)

Summary

In this chapter we have made explicit ways in which images of teaching from one generation infiltrate and subsequently become embedded in contemporary texts of teaching. What has characterized this analysis of the primary texts of schooling and the texts of cultural production has been the degree to which these texts heroize and romanticize teachers. In drawing on the semiotic work of Angela McRobbie on the code of femininity, we have identified and isolated codes and conventions of upper case R Romance and teaching: 'if I were to suddenly take over the class . . . ', 'if the regular teacher suddenly took ill . . . ', 'if only a new/beautiful/young/imaginative teacher were to take over . . .'. What are the contributions of such romantic texts to the evolution of class-rooms as gendered landscapes? What is their impact on teacher identity? In the two chapters which follow, we engage in a close reading of upper case R Romance teachers in two gendered genres in order to probe the significance of gender to the professional identity of teachers. Our focus will be the text of action hero through a reading of Arnold Schwarzenegger in *Kindergarten Cop*, and the text of desire-romance (small 'r' romance) through a reading of Barbie.

6 Action Heroes in the Classroom: The Gendered Landscape of Schooling

'They're 6-year-olds. How much trouble can they be?' (John Kimble, *Kindergarten Cop*)

What if one day your school was turned into an undercover site for a police investigation? What if your regular kindergarten teacher was conveniently removed from her teaching duties, and when you went into school the next day, there stood Mr. Kimble, a.k.a. Arnold Schwarzenegger, a.k.a. star of *Terminator 1* and *2*, a.k.a. Mr. Universe, Mr. World and Mr. Olympia? As the reviewers of the movie *Kindergarten Cop* agree, it's pretty far-fetched! Which part of the above scenario, however, is the most far-fetched — that a school could be an undercover site? Such a thing could happen, couldn't it? Is it the fact that a kindergarten teacher could actually be taken off her assignment and replaced by a person who has never gone through a teacher education program, and has no teaching experience? This is not necessarily a novel idea for Hollywood, since, as we discussed in the previous chapter, Hollywood teachers are conventionally outsiders. Is it the fact that the teacher is male? This, too, is not a novel idea for Hollywood, where generally the majority of lead roles calls for males, and where, within the genre of teacher movies, the likelihood that the teacher will be male is high (*To Sir With Love, Dead Poets Society, Blackboard Jungle, Teachers*). No, the real novelty, the Hollywood-writ-large part, is Arnold Schwarzenegger himself. Could there be anything more unlikely than a body-builder-turned-terminator-turned-cop becoming a kindergarten teacher?

In 'real' life, kindergarten teachers consider themselves to be pretty ordinary and unglamorous. It is not uncommon to hear women who teach in the early grades say 'Oh, I'm just a teacher'. Hollywood seems to agree with them — there are remarkably few references to early childhood and primary grades in movies about school. But, as we see in such books as *Schooling in the Light of Popular Culture* (Farber, Provenzo and Holm, 1994) and *Images of Schoolteachers in Twentieth-Century America* (Joseph and Burnaford, 1994b), there is no lack of movies about teachers in higher grades. Movies about school even include a good representation of Hollywood blockbusters, from *To Sir With Love* to *Blackboard Jungle* to *The Prime of Miss Jean Brodie* to *Dead Poets Society*, along with a plethora of teenage movies about schools and

94

teachers such as *Fame, Footloose, Flashdance, Breakfast Club.* Teachers in elementary school classrooms, by contrast, are usually conspicuous by their absence. Moreover, in the few films where elementary teachers do figure, the action takes place primarily outside the school setting. Thus, when a major Hollywood film sets most of the action inside a kindergarten classroom and within the hallways of an elementary school, we are witnessing a special event, something that stands out and demands to be noticed.

According to Gamman and Marshment (1989), men and women are offered society's dominant definitions of themselves through popular culture. These definitions can be challenged, nonetheless; popular culture can be viewed as a:

> site of struggle . . . it is not enough to dismiss popular culture as merely serving the complementary systems of capitalism and patriarchy, peddling 'false consciousness' to the duped masses. It can also be seen as a site where meanings are contested and where dominant ideologies can be disturbed. (*Ibid*, p. 1)

The film *Kindergarten Cop* is a good example of such a site. It disturbs and ruptures precisely because it is Arnold Schwarzenegger who plays the role of the kindergarten teacher. In this chapter, we are interested in Arnold Schwarzenegger-as-cultural text for two reasons: First, as text of action-hero turned teacher, he offers viewers a counter-text to the commonplace smaller-than-life non-heroes that construct an image of male teachers as goons, nerds, and buffoons. Second, his authoritarian macho pedagogy constitutes a striking counter-text to what has frequently been described as the 'feminized' classroom — a notion based on romantic female images and stereotypes of female teachers as 'leading-from-behind' to implement child-centered models of nurturing and caring.

Arnold Schwarzenegger: 'Action Hero Teacher'

Why does *Kindergarten Cop* work as a film? As Kindergarten Cop, does Arnold Schwarzenegger rupture, disturb, or reinforce the culture's dominant definition of elementary school teachers? We first came up against these questions while viewing the movie with a group of education students who were about to begin their final practicum experience before becoming certified as kindergarten and elementary school teachers.

In the opening scenes of the movie, we meet undercover police officer, John Kimble, a 12-year veteran of the Los Angeles Police Department who has a reputation for getting things done. For the last four years, he has been on the trail of a killer and suspected drug dealer, Cullen Crisp, whose ex-wife is apparently living incognito in a small suburban town in Oregon. Following a shoot-out murder involving the drug dealer and an informant, Kimble manages, with some difficulty, to get a female witness to identify Crisp in a police line-up. Consequently, for a short period of time, Crisp is behind bars. Kimble is of the opinion that if he could find the drug dealer's wife he could get her to testify and have enough evidence to get a conviction, putting the drug dealer behind bars for many years. The only tip that he has to go on, however, is the fact that the woman is living in Astoria and has a kindergarten-age son.

Kimble, who is a loner, finds out that he must share the assignment with another undercover officer, Phoebe O'Hara (played by Pamela Reed). The plan is that Phoebe, a former kindergarten teacher, will discover the identity of the drug dealer's son by assuming the role of a substitute teacher in his school. John, meanwhile, is supposed to track down the drug dealer's wife and get her testimony. There are complicating factors to this assignment, at least from Kimble's point of view. For example, he resents sharing this case with anyone, especially Phoebe O'Hara, since he already has little confidence in her ability as an undercover agent. Indeed, through a telling camera-shot of the police line-up scene, we see a glare exchanged between the two, with Kimble being triumphant. Moreover, Phoebe has done an un-cop-like thing by offering to make the witness a dinner if she would agree to go to the police line-up, a breach of professionalism duly noted by John. Further, there is an implied trivialization of the significance of Phoebe's prior experience as a kindergarten teacher (hence John's line 'They're 6-year-olds. How much trouble can they be?').

While they are flying to Oregon to begin their assignment, we get a foreshadowing of how unsuitable Kimble is for a kindergarten classroom. Several kindergarten-age children sit near them on the airplane. Their kicking and squirming cause Kimble to utter some rather drastic threats, a response more appropriate for drug dealers than little children. Of course, as had to happen, Phoebe falls ill on the way to Astoria, forcing Kimble to pose instead as the kindergarten teacher.

As we anticipate, the children in Kimble's classroom are rambunctious and do not at first respond to Kimble's whistle-blowing drill sergeant tactics. Much of the humour of the film derives from muscle-bound Kimble's inability to control the class, something noted by Saturday Evening Post reviewer Maynard Good Stoddard (1991):

> The teacher's got the muscle, but the kids are in control . . . Arnold Schwarzenegger flexing his bulging biceps in a kindergarten classroom easily conjures up the image of the proverbial bull in a china shop. Schwarzenegger, however, will not be making a shambles of the 5-year-old's classroom; rather, the 5-year-olds will be making a shambles of him. (p. 58)

Soon, however, Kimble is able to 'get them into shape', even physically — after all, he *is* Arnold Schwarzenegger, known for his body building and fitness campaigns! Moreover, he has the children surprise the whole school by presenting a rendition of Lincoln's Gettysburg address to an assembly of parents. Along the way, Kimble also ends up becoming romantically involved with Joyce (played by Penelope Ann Miller), one of the 'real' teachers on staff, who, as it turns out, is also the drug dealer's ex-wife, the woman for whom he has been searching. Eventually the drug dealer shows up in Astoria and tries to take his son hostage. Following a final shoot out, there is an 'all's well that ends well' finish. Order is restored, and Kimble and Joyce become a couple. The 'pedagogical finale' shows Kimble being offered a teaching position by Miss Schlowski, the Principal, who by the end of the movie is cheering him on from the standpoint of a fan rather than from the position of school administrator.

We showed this film to a seminar group of twenty-eight student teachers, only two of whom were male. Our female students, the ones who actually might become kindergarten teachers some day, could never even aspire to the hero space of John Kimble. The two men in our class were reminded that the notion of male superhero elementary teacher is something so bizarre and comical that it can easily become the subject of a Hollywood role-reversal fantasy, akin to the genre of 'men-impersonating-women' films (for example, *Tootsie, Mr. Mom, Three Men and a Baby, Mrs. Doubtfire*). If *Kindergarten Cop* had a female protagonist, the dramatic effect would be entirely lost. It would be more like a documentary on kindergarten teaching. A woman teaching kindergarten? Nothing dramatic about that! As Farber, *et al.* (1994) note, the ordinary everyday occurrences of women-as-mothers, or women-as-kindergarten-teachers become Hollywood movie scripts when the roles are played by men. What makes the film spectacular is the outrageous and unlikely appearance of a *male* kindergarten teacher.

It is not only Kimble's gender that challenges common images of kindergarten teachers. The classroom that Kimble takes over is initially arranged and furnished, like most typical North American kindergartens, to facilitate a play and activity-based pedagogy. Immediately, however, Kimble imposes his own need for order and discipline. In the opening classroom scene, he interrogates the children in order to try to identify Dominique, the child he was there to find: 'I am going to ask you some questions and I want you to answer them immediately.' When this line of questioning fails, he tries another one: each child must do a 'show and tell' on 'who is my daddy and what does he do?' John fails miserably at establishing rapport. He is not good at 'child talk', and so falls back on what he knows — police drills. Resorting to the use of a police whistle as a form of control, he soon has the children lining up and performing police marches. His teacher-directed pedagogy becomes even more apparent at the school assembly when Kimble's class performs a rendition of Lincoln's Gettysburg Address. Although the audience, (mostly parents), give the children a round of applause, ultimately it is Kimble, not the children who receives the standing ovation. This is no 'leading from behind' pedagogy. As Mark Kermode (1991) in his review of the film for *Monthly Film Bulletin* observes:

Particularly irritating is the push button transformation scene in which Kimble magically wins the support and respect of the class (though worse still is the liberty play which he teaches the children to perform for the annual fair, with much spouting of democracy). (p. 47)

Far from being a radicalizing type of rupturing, Kimble's pedagogy disturbs our usual conceptions of kindergarten with a throw-back to teacher as ultimate authority, male in power (even the female principal backs off), marching the kids around as though they were in a 1950s boot camp. Kermode (1991) makes the following comments on Kimble's 'lawman' techniques:

The scene . . . of the principal's delight in Kimble's strong-arm way of dealing with one unpleasant parent should have provided a fleeting hearty laugh. But Reitman kills the joke by stretching it over an entire scene and turning it into a paean to the lawman's potential as a teacher. (p. 47)

Kindergarten Teacher? Gendering the Disturbance

In a sense, *Kindergarten Cop* is based on an interrogation of gender roles, through the use of role reversals (male kindergarten teacher, and female Principal). This interrogation of gender also comes through the lengthy scene given over to 'who is your daddy and what does he do' which elicits comments like 'My daddy is a gynaecologist and he looks at vaginas and penises all day long'; and 'Our mom says that our dad is a real sex machine'. At one point we also learn that John Kimble was married and has a son whom he rarely sees. A violent scene involving the drug dealer, Cullen Crisp, trying to find a present for his son whom he never sees, further adds to this interrogation of gender roles.

We can see Kimble's role in the kindergarten classroom as a rupturing of everything we expect about kindergarten teachers because he is portrayed as *everything that kindergarten teachers are not*:

(i) they are not sexy;
(ii) they are not men;
(iii) they are not powerful;
(iv) they are not glamorous;
(v) they are not really authority figures;
(vi) they are not strong;
(vii) they are not heroes;
(viii) they are not leaders;
(ix) they are not tough.

Moreover, most real-life kindergarten teachers are trained professionals. How is it that Mr. Kimble is able to walk into a classroom and take over, when most people (women) need to study for many years to become kindergarten teachers? Teacher education is of so little consequence in the movie that Mr. Kimble, who has been replacing a trained teacher with twenty-five years of experience, is ultimately offered a regular teaching position in the school. Moreover, it is clear that the Principal would be quite willing to turn her administrative position over to him, even though research on gender and leadership would suggest that she must have worked very hard to get the position in the first place.

Another cinematic version of this devaluing of the teaching profession occurs in the movie *The Prince of Tides* where teacher Tom Wingo (played by Nick Nolte) decides to return to the classroom (coaching). One of the reasons that he has not been teaching even though he trained as a teacher, is that his mother thought that teaching wasn't a prestigious enough position. This point is also put forth by Mr. Dadier, a teacher in Evan Hunter's (1984) novel, *The Blackboard Jungle*, when he comments on the people who enrol in teacher training courses at universities:

> The simpering female idiots who smiled and agreed with the instruc-
> tor, who imparted vast knowledge gleaned from profound observa-
> tion made while sitting at the back of the classroom in some ideal high
> school in some ideal neighbourhood while an ideal teacher taught
> ideal students. (Hunter, 1953/1984)

Another pedagogical issue raised by *Kindergarten Cop* is the taken-for-grantedness of certain everyday aspects of teaching. Although we see Kimble working hard at school to get the children ready for the school assembly, we do not see him engaged between classes in preparing for his teaching. We are once again reminded that in Hollywood teacher films,

> 'the great majority of more ordinary relationships — both problematic
> and decent — between students and teachers in schools, and espe-
> cially the work of women in education, are simply not worth noticing.
> The ordinary is irrelevant in schooling'. (Farber *et al.*, 1994, p. 171)

Kimble's behaviour also contrasts with the notion that kindergarten teachers are supposed to have infinite patience. Arnold explodes in absolute rage when the children run uncontrollably around the classroom. He screams 'SHADDUP' out of frustration and helplessness, and then runs out of the school.

Arnold Schwarzenegger-as-Text

How does Arnold Schwarzenegger-as-text contribute to our understanding of the gendered landscape of schooling? The combination of *Kindergarten Cop*'s far-fetched story-line and Schwarzenegger's own stardom offers us an ideal cultural text for interrogating gender and teaching in the elementary class-room. As Denise Farran (1990) observes:

> ... there should be more exploration of how cultural images are actually assembled and how they have meaning in individual experi-ence. For example, Marilyn Monroe is still a figure strongly present in popular culture: what are the elements of this image? how is this constructed? why is it such a powerful image? and just as importantly, how do people in different situations, with different biographies, ex-perience this image? ... It is only through analytic examination of the complexity of how such cultural images 'work' that we can fully understand them and the hold they have over us. (p. 272)

In the *Current Biography Yearbook of 1991*, Arnold Schwarzenegger is described as

> the world's most popular movie star ... his unflagging toil, unquench-able self-confidence, and engaging media-savvy personality have ena-bled him to emerge from an obscure Alpine Village to become the world's most famous of all musclemen (he appeared on no fewer than five magazine covers in June 1990 alone). He is known for playing a particular strong man in such films as *Conan the Barbarian, The Terminator, Commando, Predator, Total Recall, Terminator 2, Judge-ment Day, Twins, True Lies* — and of course, *Kindergarten Cop*. He describes himself as 'a stamp' — I have a certain value and it has to be respected. (p. 502)

The director of *Conan the Barbarian* describes Arnold as embodying the 'Superior Man', 'the Nietzschean Man', 'There's something wonderfully prime-val about him, harking back to the real basic foundational stuff: steel and strength and will' (*ibid*). He first came to North America in 1968 to participate in the Mr. Universe contest, and although not successful then, in 1970 went on to win the titles of Mr. World, Mr. Universe and Mr. Olympia. Since that time he has produced body-building documentaries such as *Pumping Iron*, has written a number of best-selling books on bodybuilding, and more recently went on to head up President Bush's Council on Fitness and Sport.

Arnold Schwarzenegger thus exists as a larger-than-life cultural text in his own right. Journalists draw on the details of his life to support this thesis. Arnold the body-builder from nowhere becomes one of the most famous body-builders, one of the richest box office idols, and one of the most sought after stars. He admits that romanticized images drew him to America from Austria — he came in search of 'huge cars, the '57 cadillacs with their wide wings, the freeways, the whole idea of America. It was bigger than life!' (Klein, 1988, p. 41). Journalists also refer extensively to his larger than life physical measurements — the dimensions of his biceps (twenty-two inches when fully flexed), his chest measurements (fifty-seven inches) his weight, his intimidating muscles, and photos of him lifting rocks. All of this suggests that *Kindergarten Cop* cannot easily exist apart from the Arnold Schwarzenegger 'machine'. This machine includes Schwarzenegger's own confident and self-parodic personality, his involvement in body-building and physical fitness, along with all the *Conan the Barbarian, Terminator*-type movies in which he has starred.

Journalist Richard Corliss (1990) points out the connection between Schwarzenegger-as-text and Ninja Turtle action heroes based on their similar origin: 'Like a Ninja Turtle conceived in disaster and destined for greatness . . .' (p. 53). His 'sensitive guy' films, for example, *Twins* and *Kindergarten Cop*, play on this body-building text. In the film *Last Action Hero*, the hero text becomes life itself as Schwarzenegger essentially plays and parodies himself as an action hero. For example, he goes into a video store to check out the Schwarzenegger section. His name also appears on a film marquee as part of the plot of the film! Further evidence of this intertextuality can be seen in *Kindergarten Cop* when Kimble/a.k.a. Schwarzenegger lectures the children about their poor physical fitness: 'You kids are soft . . . You're not disciplined.' The advertising trailer for *Kindergarten Cop* picks up this notion of Arnold as text, using references to earlier movies: 'He's the meanest, toughest cop on the streets . . . now you can tell him you haven't done your homework'.

The Boys' Room: Action Heroes as a Counter-Text to the Feminized Classroom

As we observed in chapter 3, a number of scholars have looked at the ways that gender constructs relationships in the classroom (for example, Best, 1983; Davies, 1989; and Walkerdine, 1990). This work has been significant because it has problematized gender rather than suggesting that school necessarily privileges either males or females. At the same time, however, scholars such as Jane Miller (1992), Heather-Jane Robertson (1993), Sue Askew and Carol Ross (1988), and Christine Skelton (1989) remind us that there remains a less specified but more insidious counter-discourse around the issue of what is often disparagingly referred to as the 'feminized classroom'. The disparaging of the feminized classroom is upheld by Hollywood where, as Farber *et al.* (1994) point out:

> In virtually every case, we see a man, some sort of renegade or out-
> sider enter hostile territory, find a way to earn the trust and respect of
> students, and build bonds with them which make some tangible vic-
> tory possible. Meddlesome antagonists are clearly identified in the
> process and rebuffed in the end, though in most cases, not before
> they manage to bring the hero to despair over ever making a differ-
> ence or finishing the job he (or she) has set out to do . . . women

either act as obstacles to the work of charismatic men (as in the examples of the head of the math department whom Jaime Escalante must overcome and the villain trying to derail Joe Clark) or find their place offering comfort and support to the heroes at moments of weakness and need (as does Escalante's wife and Clark's assistant principal). (pp. 168 and 171)

As Miller (1992) observes:

Fear of women's influence as teachers and of girls' academic success at school is by no means a new fear, and its contemporary manifestations are unprecedented only in so far as they are disguised by the apparent even-handedness of current educational discourse on the subject. 'He' and 'she', like so much 'equal opportunities rhetoric' can operate to deny specific and telling differences in teaching, curriculum, management and academic outcomes in the debates and documents accounting for them. (p. 1)

Miller (1992) goes on to cite the report of a superintendent from New Jersey from the late nineteenth century who objected to women in the classroom:

I am strongly in the opinion that the presence of women as teachers of boys in the upper grammar grades, and even in the first and second year of the high school causes thousands of boys to become disgusted with and to leave the schools. Of my own knowledge, many young men have been driven from school because of their intense dislike to being (using their own words) bossed by women. (p. 4)

In *Kindergarten Cop*, this counter-discourse of devaluing female teachers by heroizing male teachers can be read in the speech of the Principal at the school assembly who gushingly praises Kimble in a manner she never uses when speaking of the other female teachers. A similar counter-text is implied by the comments made by the students' mothers who all remark on the positive significance of having a male (and single) kindergarten teacher in their children's school.

The film *Kindergarten Cop* also enters into a discourse/counter discourse about males as role models in the elementary school, particularly for boys from female-headed single parent families. Do we need more male teachers as role models? Perhaps this question needs to be problematized and reframed. What kind of male role models? Do we need Mr. Kimbles? Or do we need more teachers who can provide alternative male role models (i.e., soft, caring, student centred, nurturing individuals)? Goodman and Kelly (1988) argue that

'physical presence is not enough. The need is not for men who simply pass on the traditional male-centred culture unproblematically. To make a significant difference, we need more men who mediate culture from an anti-sexist perspective . . . as profeminist'. (p. 1)

Coulter and McNay (1994) take up this question in a careful review of the literature on male elementary teachers, pointing out that much of the discourse makes only a common sense argument, unsupported by research.

Finally, the counter-discourse of *Kindergarten Cop* is consistent with or mirrors what advertisers and Hollywood prime time producers already know: if you want to sell a product or program to boys, you need male characters. This is evident in almost all aspects of popular culture. As marketers know, if you want boys to watch a show featuring teacher characters, regardless of whether this image is positive or negative, the teacher should probably be male. Many of the successful prime time teacher television shows directed at both males and females such as *Wonder Years, Boy Meets World,* and *The Simpsons* are more likely to contain male teachers than female teachers. *The Simpsons* is particularly noteworthy because it is Mr. Skinner, the Principal, who is the important school figure rather than any one (female) teacher. Similarly, regular morning shows for both male and female preschool audiences such as *Sesame Street, Mr. Rogers,* and *Barney and Friends* involve almost exclusively male protagonists, either through the use of male puppets or live characters. While there is some question as to whether any of the Mr. Rogers-types are really teachers, they do perform a teacher function. As Ellen Seiter (1993) observes:

> Big Bird and Bert and Ernie dominate *Sesame Street.* All of the be-loved monsters are male: Snuffalupagus, Honkers, Grover, Cookie Monster. The two females in residence on *Sesame Street,* Betty Lou and Prairie Dawn, are human-looking muppets rather than more fan-ciful creatures and tend to be strictly bound to realistic, rather than fantastic actions and story lines, as though the celebrated creativity of *Sesame Street's* writers and puppeteers dried up when confronted with female heroines. (p. 149)

Seiter (1993) notes that the context for considering the viewing habits of boys and girls is such that, while girls will watch male adventures in westerns, detective stories and action hero dramas, boys are not interested in female adventures in romances and family sagas. This was born out by ABC's cancel-lation of the television cartoon show *Barbie and her Friends* in favour of keeping *Space Invaders,* not apparently for reasons of 'political correctness' in the adult world, but rather, because boys wouldn't watch *Barbie,* but girls would watch *Space Invaders* (Globe and Mail, 1990). Kim Reynolds (1990) talks about the fact that historically, girls have been willing to read stories featuring exclusively male characters, but boys have been very reluctant to read romances or stories which contain only female characters. For example, while many girls admit to reading *Nancy Drew* mysteries as well as the *Hardy*

Boys, males will seldom read (or at least admit to reading) *Nancy Drew* (Mitchell and Reid-Walsh, forthcoming). This preference for (or marketing towards) males over females can also be seen in the commercial world. As Seiter (1993) notes:

> Designers of children's commercials and promotional campaigns have also preferred male characters. The roster of mascots is entirely male: Captain Crunch (cereal); Tony the Tiger (Frosted Flakes); the elves Snap, Crackle, and Pop (Rice Krispies); Sugar Bear (Super Golden Crisp); Ronald McDonald; Geoffrey Giraffe (Toys 'R' Us). Conventional wisdom in the advertising business has it that a female trademark for a children's product will immediately turn away every boy in the audience; their belief is repeatedly proven to them by market research. (p. 149)

The absence of women (teachers) in the action figure world of boys' Saturday morning cartoons, and play world is thus not surprising.

Provenzo (1991) has pointed out that action figures, programs, and video games are in the private sector; they are not marketed towards, public school, or library services where they might be scrutinized closely. Because most parents and teachers know little about their content, the potency and appeal of these action texts increase further, offering boys a sort of 'boys room' that females (girls or female teachers) are unlikely to enter. Both Marsha Kinder (1991) and Provenzo (1991) have noted that parents and grandparents, armed with a checkbook or a credit card, often take a 'what can you do' attitude, and simply buy the action figure packages. In a sense, then, as Seiter (1993) observes, boys' play and popular culture is less likely to be mediated by the adults in their lives, especially mothers and female teachers. Girls may not have quite the same privacy. Mothers and female teachers may not approve of *Barbie* or *My Little Pony* or other girls' texts, but from their own experience, they at least know what they are about. The 'girls room' is thus more vulnerable to adult intervention because it is better known.

Many of the studies of gender stereotypes in children's literature focus on texts that are less likely to be read by males. Consequently, a point that is often missed is that, *Power Rangers* aside, women are almost totally absent from boys' texts such as the *Ninja Turtles* or *Hardy Boys*. When women do appear, it is more often as victims to be rescued, vague mothers hovering in the background, or hysterical aunts, than as empowered or interesting individuals. Thus, while the images of women in popular texts are important in terms of how they relate to the lives of girls and women, they merely serve as 'the presence of absence' in the lives of boys.

Teacher Identity in the Feminized Classroom

When Mr. Kimble loses control of the children in one of the scenes in *Kindergarten Cop*, some boys begin taunting one of the other boys in the class, calling him 'Mr. Poo-poo Head'. They do not, however, go so far as to taunt their male teacher. Such was not the fate of a female teacher in a real-life scene reported by Valerie Walkerdine (1990). In that episode, too, a group of young boys resort to taunting, using 'bathroom' language; their target, however, was their teacher.

> *Terry*: Yeah, and take your bum off, take your wee-wee off, take your clothes off, your mouth off.
>
> *Sean*: Take your teeth out, take your head off, take your hair off, take your bum off. Miss Baxter, the paxter knickers taxter. (p. 4)

Are male elementary teachers subject to this sort of belittling? What passes as 'boys will be boys' resistance might be played out differently depending upon whether boys are in the company of a male or female teacher. Robert Connell (1989) discusses school's role in shaping masculinity:

> Schools have often been seen as masculinity-making devices. Dr. Arnold saw his renovated Rugby as a means of forming a Christian gentleman. Other reformers in the years since have given schools the task of forming a sober and industrious working man, a technocratic competitor and the New Society Man . . . Schools do not simply adapt to a natural masculinity among boys or femininity among girls. They are agents in the matter, constructing particular forms of gender and negotiating relations between them. (pp. 291–2)

Because of its particular spin on the feminized classroom, *Kindergarten Cop* is of significance to females who teach in early childhood and elementary education. As Biklen (1994) notes:

> Fictional narratives participate in the cultural construction of women who teach. They do so not only directly, as stories or novels read by individuals, but also indirectly, as representations that circulate among people who call forth these images when they speak, write, or think about teachers. I take culture to mean 'the process through which we circulate and struggle over the meanings of our social experience, social relations, and therefore our selves. (p. 5)

We have said little, however, about the many male elementary school teachers who do exist and who are the object of recruitment in employment equity programs. *Kindergarten Cop* could be significant to men who consider careers in elementary teaching, shaping their internal conception of men who teach. For example, what does it mean to be the only adult male in a building full of women and children? What does it mean to be labelled 'gay', as Mr. Kimble is on the first day of school simply because he chooses to work with young children?

As we observed in the previous section, boys have contact with teacher figures through popular culture, based on Hollywood's notion of what sells. Boys do not encounter many real-life male teacher models in their elementary schools. Moreover, the culture of male childhood play does little to socialize men into elementary teaching. For example, men who do choose to become elementary school teachers are less likely to report having engaged in activities such as playing school when they were young. When boys do play school, they are more likely to assume the stance of pupils than to act as teacher. Women who report having played school as young children often mention that they taught younger brothers, and they often avail themselves of the many play-school artefacts marketed to girls. Play-school products which target boys are more likely to be of the genre of 'the little professor', a computer maths game.

As we argue in the next chapter, even the yearly 'back to school' phenomenon in catalogues, department store flyers, and magazines is commodified primarily in terms of girls rather than boys. Thus, males who choose elementary school teaching have not been socialized into the teacher role through their childhood play or popular culture in the manner that females have. We see the kind of identity conflict that this can induce in the following comments made by a male elementary preservice teacher about his drawing of a teacher:

> What to draw? What does a teacher look like? Like anybody else, I guess. What sex is a teacher? I might have originally drawn a woman, *since my brain tells me that a teacher is female*, but I wanted also to strike a blow for male equality. I wanted to make a conscious effort to overcome stereotypes (how else are we to get around these except by conscious effort?). (italics added)

Moreover, as we have illustrated previously, it is not as though all of the images of male elementary teachers are necessarily larger-than-life positive action hero images. Indeed, Mr. Kimble ruptures and disturbs precisely because he is also a counter-text to the line-up of blustering fools, goons, and irrational, smaller-than-life males in popular culture schools, for example, the teacher in the book *Thomas' Snowsuit* (Robert Munsch), Mr. Phillips in *Anne of Green Gables* (Lucy Maud Montgomery), and Mr. Skinner (*The Simpsons*).

The pedagogy of Kimble's classroom is in direct conflict with much of the child-centred pedagogy that has been supported by educational research and curriculum documents over the last fifteen years in elementary school classrooms in North America, Britain and Australia. Mr. Kimble is a hero who manages to get his kindergarten class in line in much the same way that he wraps up yet another crime in his role as an undercover police officer. Indeed, when he introduces the game of 'police school' to his students, urging them to toughen up, he states: 'You're mine now. You belong to me.' The model that Mr. Kimble sets might be seen as problematic for male teachers who try to implement a more child-centred pedagogy. As teacher Rick Dadier observes in the novel *The Blackboard Jungle*, one might expect this kind of 'intuitive nurturing thing' with females, but males need to be serious about their job:

> He had wanted to teach, had honestly wanted to teach. He had not considered the security, or the two-month vacation, or the short hours. He had simply wanted to teach, and he had considered teaching a worth-while profession. He had, in fact, considered it the worthiest profession. He had held no illusions about his own capabilities. He could not paint, or write, or compose, or sculpt, or philosophize deeply, or design tall buildings. He could contribute nothing to the world creatively, and this had been a disappointment to him until he'd realized he could be a big creator by teaching. For here were minds to be sculptured, here were ideas to be painted, here were lives to shape. To spend his allotted time on earth as a bank teller or an insurance salesman would have seemed a waste to Rick. Women, he had reflected, had no such problem. Creation had been given to them as a gift, and a woman was self-sufficient within her own creative shell. A man needed more, which perhaps was one reason why a woman could never understand a man's concern for the job he had to do. So Rick had seized upon teaching, had seized upon it fervently, feeling that if he could take the clay of undeveloped minds, if he could feel this clay in his hands, could shape this clay into thinking, reacting, responsible citizens, he would be creating. (Hunter, 1953/1984, pp. 134–5)

Kindergarten Cop says a great deal to male teachers about teachers' work in terms of teaching as a career (no need to prepare), upward mobility (you should be thinking about becoming a principal), and what Christine Williams (1992) describes as 'the glass escalator' — the advantages for males of being in a nontraditional occupation. As we observe in the first section of this chapter, the film also perpetuates a certain joking attitude about males becoming elementary teachers. As Williams (1992) points out:

> Women working in traditionally male professions have achieved an unprecedented acceptance on popular television shows. Women are portrayed as doctors (*St. Elsewhere*), lawyers (*Cosby Show, L.A. Law*), architects (*Family Ties*) and police officers (*Cagney and Lacey*). But where are the male nurses, teachers and secretaries? Television rarely portrays men in non-traditional work roles, and when it does, that anomaly is made the central focus — and joke — of the program. A comedy series about a male elementary school teacher (*Drexell's Class*) stars a lead teacher who hates children! Yet even this negative portrayal is exceptional. When a prime time hospital drama series (*St. Elsewhere*) depicted a male orderly striving for upward mobility, the show's

writers made him a 'physician's assistant' not a nurse or a nurse prac-
titioner — the much more likely 'real life' possibility. (p. 264)

Williams' (1992) analysis is a 'cross dressing' argument that says as much
about the value of work that has been traditionally seen as feminine as it does
about opportunities for men. Indeed, the argument is similar to one which
says that Western women have achieved greater levels of liberation than men
because they have the choice of wearing dresses and skirts, or trousers, but
does not take into consideration that for men, wearing women's clothing has
been laden with images of female impersonation, parody and camp, and trans-
vestism. Men impersonate women for fun, whereas there is little that is fun
about women dressing up as men. For women, 'cross dressing' has meant the
possibility of being taken seriously, being more masculine (Barbara Streisand
in *Yentl*; Julie Andrews in *Victor, Victoria*). When Arnold Schwarzenegger
cross dresses, he imposes a 'male' pattern on a 'female' role. He is not feminized;
and hence not ridiculous, just entertaining, even heroic. Mr. Kimble reconciles
the contradiction of doing 'women's work' and being a 'real' man his way,
with whistle blowing and police school drills. Men who enter elementary
education may have to read their lives against the text of Mr. World, Mr.
Universe, Mr. Olympia, *Conan the Barbarian, Terminator*, and twenty-two
inch biceps, while trying at the same time to invoke a child-centred nurturing
pedagogy of collaborative work groups and cooperative learning.

Hollywood has mainstreamed gender for teachers by placing on the table
the question 'What if Mr. World/Terminator 1 suddenly became your kindergarten teacher?' As Allen (1993) observes of men doing traditional women's
work, 'gender is highly problematized and [these men] negotiate the meaning
of masculinity every day' (p. 114). We concur with Pearson and Rooke (1994)
that there is a need for gender studies in teacher education, so that not only
female students come into contact with issues of gender. Nor is it enough for
education students to look at 'the gender issue' only as it relates to their
subject areas of maths, science, or reading. This is an important point that
should not be lost in discussions of studies of teachers' work which have
often, as Acker (1992) and Grumet (1988) observe, 'androgynized' teachers'
voices. Too, as Connell (1989) notes, studies of gender in teacher education
should not be limited to female scholars and teachers and should not focus
exclusively on the schooling of girls and women. We have argued that Arnold
Schwarzenegger as a popular culture action hero text in the film *Kindergarten
Cop* has served as a gendered site of interrogation for both males and females
who choose to become elementary teachers. In the chapter which follows, we
extend our interrogation of gender and teacher identity to Barbie as a cultural
text.

7 Teacher as Woman, Woman as Teacher: Texts of Desire

For many years, like many other women, I was a schoolgirl. I don't simply mean in the years of my formal schooling, but long after I had left my secondary school. And I mean more even than that at the point of leaving school I swapped one classroom for another, as a primary school teacher, or even that on entering the academy to teach I was still learning. I mean that the view I held of myself, one with which I have grappled for many years . . . was of a struggling little girl. Though I might appear a powerful woman to the world, this did little to change the way which I, like many other women, was infantilized, hated it and yet was terrified of the powerful woman so pejoratively set out in so many spaces, so many fictionalized spaces . . . (Walkerdine, 1990, p. xiii)

Our interrogation in chapter 6 of the box office success of 'cross dressing' in a kindergarten classroom served to expose many of the dominant images of elementary teachers, not the least of which is the conventional notion that teaching young children is something women do. In this chapter, we shift our focus away from Hollywood's larger-than-life hero images of teachers (mostly male), to representations of the everyday: female teachers doing 'women's work'. How is the ordinariness of women's work as teachers represented and negotiated in the popular culture of childhood? What is the significance of girls' and women's everyday popular culture to the struggle for teacher identity?

An integral part of female popular culture is the text of romance. In posing the above questions, we therefore examine the romance genre in the domestic play-texts of girls, looking at what Christian-Smith (1993) and others call 'texts of desire', and what Aitken (1990) describes as lower case, or 'small r' romance texts. We thus use the word 'romance' in this chapter to refer (usually) to its more everyday, 'small r' sense of romantic love and desire, including all the elements of the heterosexual love story — the passions of a Romeo for a Juliet, secret yearnings, swooning maidens, broken hearts, and declarations of undying love. We also consider, as texts of romance and desire, same-sex love, crushes, and teachers' pets.

In their actual day-to-day teaching, teachers are not usually romanticized (in either the upper or lower case sense of the word). Nevertheless, we argue, the text of teacher identity cannot be separated completely from the texts of gender, love, and sexuality. Although everyday life does not always involve romance and sex, it does surround or confront us with a wide array of popular small 'r' romance texts such as soap operas, magazines, novels, advertising, tabloids, and more. Moreover, whether we acknowledge it or not, the real-life classroom is a 'sexuated space', and teaching is a gendered enterprise that, at times, involves love, passion, power, and desire. In offering a reading of women teachers through the lens of romance texts, we provide a framework for reconsidering the professional identity and work of teachers. To begin our investigation of romantic representations of woman-teacher, we have chosen an unlikely, but effective point of entry — Barbie.

When Barbie Goes to School

A window display of Barbie dolls in a Tel Aviv toy store prompts us to enter. We are in Israel to attend a conference and we take advantage of this opportunity to explore children's popular culture in a country unfamiliar to us. We had already visited a bookstore where we discover Sweet Valley High and Nancy Drew books translated into Hebrew. Now this huge display of Barbie artefacts beckons. Inside, we see a group of young women who look no more than 17 or 18 years of age. They are 'oohing' and 'aahing' over the latest Barbies. They choose some to buy, and line up at the counter to pay for them. Birthday presents for younger sisters, we enquire? No, the shop owner assures us — these teenagers are buying them for themselves — something to take with them to the army as they begin their compulsory military service. (Extract from fieldnotes in a toystore, Tel Aviv, June 1993)

Barbie is one of the most pervasive texts of desire to be found in the contemporary popular culture of girlhood worldwide. In many countries, toy stores even have whole sections devoted exclusively to Barbie dolls, accesories, and spin-off products. It is possible to see young girls from Iqaluit in the North West Territories of Canada to Cathcart in South Africa playing with the same Barbie.

As a text-of-desire, Barbie quite naturally 'walked' into our research through the frequent Barbie-like representations of teachers that we noticed in young girls' drawings. Moreover, as we soon discovered, Barbie has 'dabbled in teaching' on various occasions during her 36-year history. For example, she was once sold packaged as a music teacher, accompanied by appropriate music teacher paraphernalia. One of the many career outfits that can be purchased separately for any Barbie doll is a teacher ensemble. More recently, on the cover of the 1993 November issue of *Barbie Fashion*, Barbie is featured as a teacher of geography, surrounded by apples 'for the teacher' (see figure 7).

Figure 7   Barbie is not just any student teacher

When we discovered Barbie in the role of student teacher in a Marvel *Barbie* comic episode, we realized that we had found an ideal site for beginning our interrogation of the images of women and their work as elementary teachers.

Because Barbie is so well known, her appearance as a student teacher in a comic book is not just any fictional representation, any more than Arnold Schwarzenegger, as an action hero teacher, is just any kindergarten teacher. Barbie cannot be separated from the central themes of romance, sexuality, and consumerism that she represents in the texts of girlhood play. What does it mean when Barbie is no longer merely a doll, no longer only a symbol of consumerism and sexism, but actually a teacher — 'one of us'? As Robert Leeson (1992) observes of the presence of teachers in the popular British after-school series *Grange Hill*, you know you are 'included' when you are represented in popular culture. When Barbie steps into the role of teacher, she brings into the text of teaching a text of romance, complete with its baggage of devalued status and controversy. It is necessary to explore the ways in which such romance texts construct the identity of female teachers.

On the first page of the comic story *The Art of Teaching*, we meet Barbie, a student teacher assigned to teach, not a lesson on something like maths or grammar, but one on art history! Like action hero John 'Kindergarten Cop'

Kimble, who is appropriately dressed for his first day of school, Barbie arrives at school looking like a teacher: briefcase in hand, wearing a short, but not immodest pleated skirt and a matching jacket. Her hair, although not in a bun, is neatly tied back. Not unlike Mr. Kimble, who looks rather nervous upon his first arrival at school, when Barbie reaches the door of the school, she expresses the anxiety that most beginning teachers feel:

> Today is the first day of school! Even though I've studied art appreciation for many years, I'm still a little nervous about 'student teaching.'

As Barbie makes her way through the halls of the high school, which has as its motto 'Knowledge through learning', the similarities between her and Mr. Kimble evaporate. Barbie says to herself worriedly, 'I hope I'll be a good teacher . . . and that the students learn a lot from me.' Her self-doubt is in marked contrast to the confidence of Mr. Kimble, who wonders how difficult a group of six year-olds could be anyway. Unlike the early scenes of *Kindergarten Cop*, where Kimble initially seems hopeless as a teacher, right from the beginning of the *Barbie* episode, we have every reason to believe that Barbie's students will learn. We learn that she is adequately prepared in terms of content (much better than Kimble was), because she tells us that she has studied art appreciation for many years. Indeed, we see Barbie delivering a well-organized lesson on different periods in art history. Through the use of slides, Barbie's students (and the young readers of the comic book) are introduced to Rembrandt, Monet, Picasso and Warhol. She also talks about particular movements in art, referring to realism, impressionism, cubism and pop art. Barbie has the full attention of her students, the slide projector works well, the students remain orderly. The only criticism that a university supervisor might have is that she does not involve the students in much discussion.

Through the interior thought monologues of a student, Jessica, we gain some idea of Barbie's impact. As a new student in the school, Jessica had been feeling somewhat marginalized by the girls in the Pink Sweater Club. Barbie manages to get through to Jessica, inspiring her to such an extent that she joins an after-school art club, and finds herself no longer intimidated by the Pink Sweater Club Girls. Jessica learns the value of scholarship over popularity. She thanks Barbie for helping her to 'find herself' and is surprised when she receives reciprocal appreciation from Barbie:

> *Jessica*: Me? Why would you want to thank me?
> *Barbie*: Because I love teaching . . . and helping you with your problem has been very rewarding for me.

Thus, in the final scene of this episode, Barbie reveals her true love of teaching and implicitly positions woman-as-teacher in the role of selfless and devoted nurturer.

From what we have seen thus far, Barbie seems to know the codes of popular culture teaching that we described in chapter 5. For example, she romanticizes learning, taking the students into exciting new areas of knowledge — leading right up to Andy Warhol and pop art — the popularizing of pop art! Like Alex Jurrell in the movie *Teachers*, who inspires his students to be interested in civics, or like Starlight, who provides a 'hands-on' experience with history and science, Barbie has managed to maintain the school's motto 'knowledge is learning'. In reaching her students, especially Jessica, she evokes the upper case R romantic image of teacher-as-saviour, reminiscent of Starlight in *My Little Pony*, who saves her peers from ignorance, or Mr. Dadier in *Blackboard Jungle*, who saves a generation of lost youths. In many other episodes of the same comic, Barbie seems to have this saviour quality — feeding the homeless, for example, or saving one of her sister's friends from anorexia. This saviour or saintly quality, however, is always understated; it emerges quietly, as part of the everyday, in contrast to the 'look-at-me' heroism of Mr. Kimble.

Barbie's power as teacher seems very tied up in helping her students and in saving them from themselves. As we saw in the final panel of the comic, Barbie reveals the relational concern that female teachers are supposed to have: '. . . helping you with your problem has been very rewarding for me.' Barbie's sense of identity as teacher seems closely connected to pleasing and being needed by her students.

Female teachers are supposed to be selfless and sexless, adopting a 'leading from behind', child-centred pedagogy. As Walkerdine (1990) argues, this can lock them into positions of 'pathological nurturance' — if all the students are happy and successful, then the teacher too, is happy and successful. As constraining as this nurturing stance might be to a mother of one or more children, Walkerdine maintains that to adopt an 'is everybody okay?' stance with 25 first-grade students, takes on a pathology of its own. The elementary school classroom is one of the few places where women have power, and yet if they are doing their job well, they ensure that it is the child who feels empowered.

As Britzman (1991) observes:

> In the dominant society, so-called favourable images that characterize the teacher as selfless, also mirror the stereotypes associated with women. Like the 'good' woman, the 'good' teacher is positioned as self-sacrificing, kind, overworked, underpaid, and holding an unlimited reservoir of patience . . . Such images subvert a critical discourse about the lived contradictions of teaching and the actual struggles of teachers and students. (p. 5)

This self-sacrificing image of teachers has political overtones, for, as Britzman points out, teachers are also supposed to be antiunion, and willing to do anything for the children. This is exemplified by a news item about teachers in Prince Edward Island who voted to go on strike. The headline of the news-paper reads 'Teachers Going Too Far — Murphy: What's Best for the Island is Not Always What's Best for Any One Group'. As we read on, we learn that the Agriculture minister, himself a former vice principal, sympathizes with the plight of the teachers whose salaries were abruptly rolled back 7 per cent. At the same time, however, he observes of these government employees: 'I don't think they'll go much further (with pressure tactics) because they're a pretty good bunch (implying that, after all, they're women).' (*Charlottetown Guardian*, April 29, 1994). It is not hard to imagine Barbie voting against a strike for the sake of her students.

Barbie as a Site of Interrogation: Deep Structure/ Surface Structure

In the same way that Arnold Schwarzenegger serves as a point of entry for interrogating dominant images of the elementary school teacher, particularly in terms of the gendered nature of teachers' work, Barbie serves as a point of entry for interrogating women's work as teachers, offering as she does a prac-tical example of Irigaray's (1993) observation that 'men's culture is regularly valorized and women's culture is regularly devalorized' (p. 38). As cultural texts, Arnold Schwarzenegger and Barbie serve to locate the tensions, dilem-mas and contradictions in the professional identity of teachers. However, while both might be read as 'larger-than-life', Romantic representations of beginning teachers, their similarities disappear even before they enter the classroom. Arnold, as we have argued in the previous chapter, enters the classroom as an action hero, bearing all of the 'maleness' of Hollywood action heroes. In so doing, he offers a challenge to the stereotypes of elementary teachers in gen-eral, and kindergarten teachers in particular. Arnold-as-kindergarten-cop is a superhero text, inseparable from Mr. World, Mr. Universe, and The Termina-tor. Barbie-as-teacher is not a hero text in the same way. Her work as a teacher is good, but not out of the ordinary, and her success in helping Jessica is just one of life's 'special but small' moments. No applause, no defeating of drug dealers, no shoot-outs, no sweeping of potential lovers off their feet — just 'turning them on' to art history, just the ordinary job of teaching.

But Barbie is also 'every girl's dream' of what a woman should be, or at least, she is Mattel's rendition of that dream. As the ultimate romance text, she enters the classroom laden with all the gendered stereotypes and cliches that characterize women in romance. She's beautiful, shapely, and has a dazzling smile and flawless complexion. Her measurements, much to the annoyance of her critics, set unrealistic standards of beauty, with a tiny waist and firm, ample bosom. She's young, blond, manicured, toned, sexy, and fashionably dressed. Her perfect good looks are matched by her good, yet fun-loving nature. She is adored, played with, collected, and coveted. She 'gets along' with everyone . . . everyone, that is, but her many critics.

Although she is a cultural icon to young girls all over the world, Barbie differs from Arnold Schwarzenneger in that she simultaneously occupies a universally devalued position (Mitchell and Reid-Walsh, in press). Indeed, as Richard Peabody and Lucinda Ebersole (1993) observe in their introduction to *Mondo Barbie: An Anthology of Fiction and Poetry*, Barbie remains a problem for many — a *deep* problem:

> Barbie is an American icon: the product of an adult's fantasy of a girl-child's toy. Or is Barbie the adult's toy and the child's fantasy? What happens when the adult's fantasy collides with the child's fantasy? Sparks fly. You would have no 'Angry Women' issue of RE/SEARCH without Barbie. This book is the answer to millions of prayers . . . At last revealed — all that misplaced Barbie angst, all that childhood conditioning, torture and repression. A home for brave Barbie survivors who can finally step forward. 'My name is . . . and I had a Barbie.' (p. xvi)

To mention the name 'Barbie' at almost any adult gathering is to invite derision or interrogation — a chorus of unbelieving 'oh no's'. Our families wonder what could possibly be 'academic' about Barbie, and ask how we could devote so much time, energy, and even research funds to this seemingly frivolous subject. A few of our university colleagues express similar concerns, and some of our undergraduate students squirm and look embarrassed when we bring up Barbie, only to reveal that it wasn't so long ago that they stopped playing with Barbie themselves! Even colleagues in Cultural Studies or Communications, who themselves study texts such as feminist detective fiction, Madonna, *Dallas*, *Y and R* (*The Young and the Restless*) or *Star Wars*, disparage this text of girlhood, this *doll*.

Linda Hutcheon (1989) describes the postmodern as not so much a concept as a problematic. Following Burgin (1986), she defines the problematic as 'a complex of heterogenous but interrelated questions which will not be silenced by any spuriously unitary answer' (p. 15). The 'spuriously unitary answer' that has almost always accompanied Barbie since her birth 36 years ago has been 'no' — a flat rejection of her and everything she appears to stand for (beauty, the male gaze, body, fashion, femininity, materialism, big business, and mass marketing). We argue that this spuriously unitary rejection is the same one that accompanies much of the popular culture literature for girls and women, particularly those texts which could be described as 'texts of desire' (*Harlequin* romances, *Mills and Boon* romances, soap operas, women's magazines, *Sweet Valley High* series, and much more).

On the surface, we suggest, Barbie hardly warrants the spurious 'no' she so often receives. While it is true that over the years she has been a bride, a date, a fun-loving vacationer in Hawaii, a backyard weekender with barbecues, pool parties, and tennis games, she has also had a multitude of careers, including those of astronaut, marine biologist, fashion designer, fashion model, nurse, doctor, flight attendant, ballet dancer, rockstar and, of course, teacher. Despite the meticulous professionalism she displays in all of her careers, Barbie never seems to be taken seriously. Why not? Is the dismissal really directed at Barbie dressed to teach, perform surgery, fly an airplane, or model, or is Barbie-the-stereotype the real target?

John Fiske (1989) has identified the critical reception that surrounds Barbie and other texts as a type of cultural text in itself, and as such, open to a close reading. Reading this text, it is safe to say that if any other student teacher, fictional or real, had taught Barbie's art class, they would not have been subjected to so much negative criticism. Indeed, if Arnold Schwarzenegger had taught her class, he would probably have been applauded. But Barbie is Barbie — a famous, but despised symbol of women's oppression, materialism, and sexism. She elicits ambivalence, even rejection, we argue, because her 'surface structure' as a student teacher is inseparable from her 'deep structure' as a text of desire.

Sander Gilman (1985) uses the terms 'surface structure' and 'deep structure' to talk about stereotypes of the sexualized woman in art (for example, Edouard Manet's 'Olympia' and Claude Monet's 'Nana'). Most of the features of Barbie as student teacher that we have discussed so far — her jacket and skirt, the slides, the lesson — might be regarded as surface features, the 'window dressing' of the text. Today Barbie is dressed as a teacher in the same way that yesterday she was dressed for rollerblading, and tomorrow she'll be dressed for her prom date with Ken. On the surface, Barbie appears to be the ideal student teacher. She is concerned about her lesson, has clearly planned well, attends to the individual needs of her students, and manages, despite the fact that she is Barbie, to look quite respectable for her first day of school. It would be unfair to say 'that's funny, you don't look like a teacher, Barbie'. If it's not her surface structure that provokes controversy, what then, of her deep structure?

Barbie: Text of Controversy and Contradiction

Barbie has always been controversial — each successive version of the doll has brought with it new controversies and attention to new contradictions. These merit attention, for as Gilman (1985) observes, the deep structure of controversial texts is also the deep structure of what we both fear and glorify. Barbie's most vehement critics in the early years were men who opposed her predatory behaviour. Now, her most ardent critics are women. As Stern and Schoenhaus (1990) conclude:

> Barbie has come a long way. In the 1960s she was considered a perfect bitch. Today she is regarded as a complete bimbo. (p. 63)

In either case, and over time, the criticisms may be taken as signals of the contradictions and ambiguity that can result from the interplay of deep and surface structures. We see Barbie as a sexy adult doll to be played with by little girls, as a symbol of unrealistic standards of beauty and wealth, and as a woman who miraculously 'has it all', managing to maintain a glamorous and challenging full-time career, while excelling in all manner of sports and artistic endeavours. But it doesn't even end there, for here comes Barbie of the 90s, who has a heightened consciousness regarding the environment, social justice, social action, feminism, and multiculturalism, and simultaneously retains her text of conspicuous consumerism, extended leisure, glamour, and sexuality!

An example of a Barbie controversy specifically related to schooling is the widespread outcry which accompanied the release of a talking Barbie doll that was programmed to say, among other things, 'Maths class is tough'. Educators, mathematicians, and women's groups did not react kindly to Barbie's women-aren't-good-at-maths attitude, fearing she was reinforcing stereotypes and setting a negative role model for female students. Other specific concerns have centred, not surprisingly, on the cultural text of Barbie's body which has been linked by her critics to instances of female obsession with weight and body shape, eating disorders, and low self-esteem. An extreme example of just how far a Barbie obsession can go is the case of a woman who appeared on a television talk show to explain that she had undergone extensive plastic surgery in order to have her body and face re-modelled so that she could look exactly like Barbie.

It is not our intention to 'cover over' the physical features of Barbie or the consumer world that she represents. As Ellen Seiter (1993) points out in *Sold Separately*, the mass marketing of toys and educational products from the 1940s and 50s onward signals children as part of consumer capital. Mattel's Barbie is just another piece of the Fisher-Price-Lego-type world of manufacturing empires. We contend, however, that Barbie-as-text is never 'sold separately'; she cannot be read separately from the context in which she is encountered, as a play-text, a text of women's popular culture, a text of desire. Thus, although through its surface structures, a text like the Barbie-as-teacher episode seems to offer the young reader 'licence' to have a crush on a teacher, or admire a teacher, or emulate a teacher, these texts are simultaneously derided as 'girls' stuff' — material that is ultimately not worthwhile, and must be left behind. Young girls must grapple, not only with Barbie as a toy/text, but also with that spurious 'no' they overhear from adults (perhaps even their mothers). How do girls feel about themselves, caught unaware in the interface of surface and deep structure, when they find themselves wanting, liking, valuing, and enjoying the same Barbie that respected adults say is so silly or offensive?

Selling School to Girls: Deep Text/Surface Text

Perhaps Raphael Best's (1983) observation that girls are much more likely than boys to be in tune with teachers and schooling helps explain why school sells well to girls and is therefore commodified for them. For example, every summer, the back-to-school phenomenon is prominant in department store flyers and widely-read girls' magazines such as *Seventeen*. Why is so much back-to-school marketing directed almost exclusively to girls? Even more importantly, why are girls' popular texts of schooling (such as magazines) accorded such low status? How might this affect the professional identity of women teachers?

As early as July, when the August editions of these magazines arrive on the newsstands, teachers and schooling are already figuring in the fantasies of girls. For example, Caroline Miller, editor-in-chief of *Seventeen*, made the following observations for her readers in the August 1994 issue:

> One of the weirdest things about summer is how great school looks from the safety of your beach towel. So what if a month ago you were dying to get out and could think of nothing you'd rather do than park your body by the side of a pool. By mid-July the heat has lost some of its charm, the pool is full of shrieking kids, and your arms are peeling . . . The truth is, you miss your friends, the gossip, the convenience of having so many guys within scoping range, and even the collective suffering at the hands of the algebra teacher from hell . . . All of which is enough to make anyone think fondly of school. As in fantasize about that first day. Forget chem homework, forget SAT flashcards . . . (p. 12)

In her analysis of the advertising in *Seventeen* magazine, Gunilla Holm (1994) found that school is marketed through forms of conventional femininity which, as McRobbie (1991) observes, include the codes of romance, personal/domestic life, fashion, and beauty. The ads Holm found in the August 'back to school' issues from 1966–1989 included the following sort of copy: 'This fall's required reading: fashion footnotes'; 'Go to the head of the class in smart looking shoes from Thom McAnn', and the like. In the August 1994 issue of the same magazine, we found many similar examples that link schooling to fashion, beauty, romance, or desire, showing how some things really don't change:

> Break the rules, go with your heart;
> Listen up! Is that you looking like a goddess in the front row?;
> It's 11pm, do you know what you're wearing tomorrow?;
> School stuff for people with homework: Term papers, and taste;
> We recommend an apple a day: it's our family remedy for limp, rat hair;
> Looking smart this fall is easy when the Dean's list is posted. Check it out, and make the grade in style.

The August 1994 issue of *Girls' Life*, a magazine aimed at a younger audience of girls (ages 7–11), makes the same point with it's back-to-school cover story, 'Are you popular?'.

School is also commodified for girls in other school-related romance texts such as 'secret diaries', school agendas, and calendars based on the *Sweet Valley* series or the *Baby-sitter's Club*. Still further examples include Disney's Story-Board games which draw on Sleeping Beauty and Cinderella-type fairy-tale romance texts for story-telling activities. Thus, school goes below the surface of a Power-Rangers lunch kit or pencil case (which might be marketed for both boys and girls) to artefacts that are simultaneously a popular culture text, a text of schooling (such as writing stories or journals), and a text of desire.

Sexualizing the Teacher in Popular Culture

Although there is a growing and important body of research on gender and teaching, little research in teacher education has addressed directly the tensions and dilemmas in the lives of women teachers around issues of sexuality. And yet, as the work of literary scholars such as Oram (1989) and Auchmuty (1992) illustrates, the history of women as teachers carries with it both implicit and explicit references to sexuality. The turn-of-the-century 'rules of conduct' cited in chapter 3 are a good example of how the lives of women teachers have been regulated according to their sexuality. The marriage bar during the interwar years in Britain, which ensured that women teachers were spinsters, also explicitly addressed women's sexuality in the context of their employment. At the same time, as Oram (1989) observes, unmarried women came to be seen as unfulfilled, so that teaching was seen as a substitute for motherhood:

> it was rather a contradiction, then, that single women teachers were increasingly criticized for not being actual mothers themselves, despite the fact that they would have lost their jobs or marriage in most areas. (*Ibid*, p. 103)

Thus, by the 1930s, there was concern (particularly from the medical profession) about 'old maids' teaching boys, and then concern that if these women were teaching girls, there could be 'perversions'. Sexuality and teachers may not often be spoken of in the same breath, but the links between the two have been implicitly (and sometimes explicitly) explored in popular literature and other cultural texts, especially movies. We argue that the small 'r' romance in the cumulative cultural text of teacher brings with it the same deep structure as Barbie.

Over 35 years ago, Jack Schwartz (1960) identified 81 Hollywood films that feature teachers. One of the themes running through these early movies is teacher romance. Schwartz's analysis addresses the question 'What do teachers have to do to be successful romantically?'. 'Success' was defined in terms of heterosexuality and the implication that the romance would extend beyond the end of the film. Schwartz observed that to succeed at love, film teachers frequently had to either 'love down' (fall in love with someone of a lower social class or educational background), or leave the profession altogether. Similarly, Foff (1956) wrote:

> To succeed as a teacher, one must fail as a man or woman. Little wonder that education is commonly regarded as the refuge of unsaleable men and unmarriageable women. (p. 27)

In an analysis of more recent teacher images in 28 'teen-films' released between 1980–87 for the adolescent market, Crume (1988) found that teachers were not often depicted as sexual or romantic individuals, perhaps because the focus of these films was adolescent, and not adult sexuality. The stereotype of the teacher as sexually frustrated, while not absent, was not given undue emphasis in these movies (p. 181). Nonetheless, Crume found that even in this genre of school movie, female teachers are more likely than males to be depicted as sexually active.

In our own analysis of popular Hollywood school films from 1964 to 1992, we found numerous references to romance and sexuality. For example, in the movie *To Sir With Love*, Mr. Thackeray ('Sir') is adored by his female students who thank him for taking them 'from crayons to perfume'. One of his students, Pamela, develops a serious crush on him. In addition, the possibility of interracial romance is hinted at through the developing closeness between Mr. Thackeray and an attractive female colleague. Another example is *Teachers*, which involves a romantic relationship between a male teacher and a female attorney. In *Kindergarten Cop*, almost from the very moment that John Kimble enters the school, there is an undercurrent of romance and sexual attraction.

Even more significant than the incidence of romance in these films is the 'gaze' through which scenes of romance and sexuality are depicted. The work of Laura Mulvey (1975) on the notion of 'the male gaze' in film narratives, and the work by Gamman and Marshment (1989) on the significance of 'the female gaze' in more recent Hollywood films such as *Thelma and Louise*, offer challenges to what is written or read as 'sexual' in film narratives. Gamman and Marshment (1989) take up Mulvey's interpretation of male gaze to refer to the ways

> that visual pleasure in mainstream Hollywood cinema derives from and reproduces a structure of male looking/female to-be-looked-at-ness (whereby the spectator is invited to identify with a male gaze at an objectified female) which replicates the structure of unequal power relations between men and women. (p. 5)

In films that feature teachers, the window into teacher romance and sex is usually through the male gaze. For example, in *Kindergarten Cop*, it is from the perspective of the male gaze that we see the relation between John Kimble and Joyce develop. In the final scene, where he sweeps Joyce into his arms, the camera angle makes her the one who appears exposed. It is her sexuality, more than his, that is put on display. An even more striking example is provided by one of the few female teacher protagonists in the Hollywood line up — Miss Jean Brodie. Viewed through the male gaze, her romantic and sexual life is scrutinized and laid bare. We are told repeatedly that she is 'in her prime' (sexually), we notice her penchant for tight sweaters and soft fabrics, and learn of her romantic and sexual involvements with both the art master and the music teacher. The glimpse we are given of her nightdress, a wispy silk garment, suggests just how rupturing this movie portrayal of a teacher is. Jean Brodie in her sexy nightdress would be a suitable model for the cover of this book!

Another instance of the male gaze occurs in the film *Blackboard Jungle*, when a male student attempts to rape a female teacher. We see that being a teacher offers a woman little power or protection, even from students, and doesn't prevent males from viewing her as object/victim. Dana Polan's (1993) study of film and literary images of the professoriate provides further examples of how the male gaze manipulates the viewer:

The flashy look for today's academic may not signal a new relationship to knowledge but may run the risk of saying the same old thing in public representation: namely that professor's relation to knowledge is perhaps inauthentic and an alibi for suspicious desires . . . Think for example of *Back to School* where the English professor, played by Sally Kellerman, appears an intense presence; in her first scene in the film, the professor in a vibrant red dress strides onto a stage and begins throatily to read that famous speech of female sensuality, the Molly Bloom soliloquy. (p. 40)

This sexualizing of female teachers can also be seen in television shows that depict teachers. One of the earliest sit-coms on American television, *Our Miss Brooks*, revolves around many scenes of Miss Brooks swooning over Mr. Boynton, the biology teacher, and her many attempts to get him to see her in a romantic light. In a more serious drama, an episode of *Marcus Welby MD*, an attractive young third-grade teacher, Ruth, suddenly develops a headache that is so debilitating, she loses control and strikes a child. She is subsequently examined by young Dr. Kiley who immediately diagnoses her as suffering from 'a premature case of old maid school teacher'. As it turns out, she has a brain tumour and eventually dies, but not before she and the handsome Dr. Kiley become romantically involved! Even more tellingly, one of her students, in what is meant by the scriptwriters to be a humorous remark, mistakenly refers to the 'substitute' teacher who takes Ruth's place as 'not a very good prostitute'!

The depiction of teachers as involved in romance is not limited to television shows for adults and teenagers. As Seiter (1993) observes of video cartoons for girls:

Girls' animated series in the 1980s borrowed from popular genres for adult women. In *My Little Pony,* the ethos of the soap opera — that feelings are all important — is combined with some conventions of the paperback romance . . . Like the soap opera there is an emphasis on understanding the often mysterious codes of feelings. Unlike the soap opera, the characters never appear in the domestic sphere . . . These cartoons dramatize the thrill of vulnerability found in the paperback romance, minus the romantic love. The ponies often find themselves wandering through a maze, similar to the heroine's search through the mansion in the gothic romance. (pp. 169–70)

While the child ponies may be too young to experience romantic yearnings, the adult ponies in their lives do — even the teachers. For example, in an episode called 'The hot air balloon science lesson', we see Starlight and her friends gathered in the schoolyard with Miss Hackney and a male professor, for a demonstration of aerodynamics. The professor has brought along a hot air balloon which is positioned for launching. Before the demonstration, however, he suggests to Miss Hackney that it would be nice to have a cup of tea, and Miss Hackney coyly acquiesces. There is a hint of romantic intention in the air. Predictably, the ponies embark upon adventure when they climb into the unattended balloon. While there is an 'all's well that ends well' conclusion to the episode, Miss Hackney is clearly 'not in charge' when she immediately abandons the class to accommodate the professor. An almost identical enactment of female abandonment of students occurs in *Kindergarten Cop,* when Joyce rushes across the hall to Kimble's class, leaving her own class to fend for themselves while she attends to his needs.

Of course, movies and television are not the only, or even the most usual sites for the depiction of teacher romance and sexuality. As we have indicated in previous chapters, the texts of girls' toys and play, the genre of the boys' British school story, and the genre of the school girls' story are replete with vivid images of teachers, many of which carry with them, either implicitly or explicitly, themes of romance, sexuality, and power. Indeed, one of the few areas of scholarship that has addressed sexuality and romance in schooling can be found in the work of literary scholars such as Rosemary Auchmuty (1992), Isobel Quigly (1982) and Joanathan Gathorne-Hardy (1977). As these authors highlight in their work, the school story is full of controversial allusions to the sexuality of 11- and 12-year-olds, the possibility of homosexual and lesbian love, love between a headmistress and a pupil, crushes on senior students or teachers, teachers exploiting or 'petting' their students, and sublimated passion, romance, and betrayal.

Initially, school stories featured idealized, 'larger-than-life' teachers, and romanticized learning in such a way, that it is not easy to separate upper case 'R' romance (which romances knowledge and a romantic attachment to school), from small 'r' romance (which refers more specifically to desire, sexuality, crushes and pets). As Frith (1987) notes:

the intensely romantic friendships which characterize these novels are closely linked with the joys of learning, and also depend on a secure concept of gender difference, of 'womanliness' perceived as a state so absolute that once achieved it is secure, and which can only be achieved by and through the models presented by other women. There are many idealized teachers who have consciously chosen to abjure marriage in order to devote themselves and their lives to the education of the girls, and for whom their pupils feel a strongly romantic affection. (p. 126)

Frith (1987) goes on to describe the case of Miss Thornhill in Sarah Dowdney's novel, *When We Were Young Together*:

That mouth, always to Jennet the loveliest that she had ever seen; the smile that haunted the full, red lips was indescribably dreamy and sweet. To her, Una Thornhill with her deep blue eyes and creamy skin, had the looks of an enchantress, and The Enchantress was the name by which she called her, though little guessing that by this very name Miss Thornhill had been really known in other days . . . The peculiar charm of eyes and smile which had 'enchanted' many world-worn men and women, now won the hearts of the most impressionable schoolgirls, and achieved more conquests over stubborn wills than Miss Sand could ever boast of having gained. (pp. 126–127)

A prominent aspect of 'romancing the teacher' has long been the phenomenon of the 'teacher's pet'. Wendy Luttrell (1993), for example, notes in her report of adults' memories:

Being someone's pet suggested an emotional or even erotically tinged relationship between pets and their owners (as in the common expression, 'petting'). In this individual, personal, emotional, and perhaps erotically tinged relationship between teachers and pets, a process of deception and objectification took place. Girls who participated in such relationships were seen or saw themselves as presenting a false self to attract the teacher's attention. Because the pet's achievements and school knowledge was gained through such deception, it was at once false and suspect. Thus, the women came simultaneously to long for and distrust the pet's recognition, attention and power. Last but not least, the concept of teacher's pet implied that a student was less than a teacher, the human pet being an infantilized person. Thus the pet's power was based on diminution and was ultimately self-negating. (p. 538)

Another instance of the teacher's pet phenomenon is found in the famous relationship between Jean Brodie and 'the Brodie set'. Indeed, the whole narrative of *The Prime of Miss Jean Brodie* is about pets — the Brodie set ('my girrrlls'), and the abusive power games, sexuality, and betrayals that are often associated with 'petting'.

In the work on the girls' school story genre, there are also extensive references to crushes. Auchmuty (1992), quoting Sara Burstall, author of *English High Schools for Girls* describes the crush as

> a phenomenon characteristic of girls' education — the hero worship, adoration, or schwärmerei — there is no exact English word for it — which some girls have felt, and many others have seen in others . . . toward some teacher or leader in school life. (p. 134)

Given their prevalence in the past, it should not be surprising that teacher crushes and pets still appear in the texts of schooling in contemporary children's popular culture. However, it is important to point out that such themes are now mostly seen in texts written for young girls. For example, the admiration that Jessica and Elizabeth and their friends have for Ms. Shepard, the student teacher in *Barnyard Battle*, is a type of crush. Other books in the same *Sweet Valley High* series feature female student crushes on a male teacher. Even in the *Barbie* comic, we could imagine the possibility of Jessica or some other student developing a crush on their beautiful and devoted teacher.

Like much of women's popular culture and female sexuality, these experiences are usually dismissed as unworthy of serious attention or scholarly consideration. The sexuality of female teachers is often portrayed, not as healthy or enriching, but as perversion, as dangerous. Teaching and learning, after all, are not supposed to have anything to do with sex. Any hints to the contrary must be swept under the carpet, ridiculed, blamed on woman's inherent weak nature (back to Eve and the apple again), or covered over.

Covering Over Teacher Identity

Our interest in studying the contradictions in the lives of women by interrogating the culture of girls is not without precedent. As Lyn Mikel Brown and Carol Gilligan (1992) observe in *Meeting at the Crossroads: Women's Psychology and Girls' Development*:

> From listening to girls at the edge of adolescence and observing our own and other women's responses we begin to see the outlines of new pathways in women's development and also to see the outlines of new pathways for women's involvement in the process of political change. When women and girls meet at the crossroads of adolescence, the intergenerational seam of a patriarchal culture opens. (p. 232)

Moreover, Brown and Gilligan argue that it is necessary to go even further back than adolescence to understand women's psychology. By addressing the critical points in girls' lives, we can understand more fully the lives of women.

In another essay, Gilligan (1991a) describes a type of revision and 'covering over' that seems to accompany girls as they pass from childhood to early adolescence. They begin, she notes, to revise their experiential and relational world-as-girls, labelling their own feelings and childhood experiences as 'false', or 'illogical' or 'stupid' — something to be ashamed of, rather than a source of pride:

> This act of revision washes away the grounds of girls' feelings and thoughts and undermines the transformatory potential which lies in women's development by leaving girls-turning-into-women with the sense that their feelings are groundless, their thoughts are about nothing real, what they experienced never happened, or at the time they could not understand it. (p. 7)

The notion of 'covering over' may account for many of the dilemmas and contradictions in the lives of women, both as teachers and as learners. This is illustrated by the position occupied by the teachers in Brown and Gilligan's study. While the teachers' conscious intention is to offer a supportive and encouraging environment to adolescent girls, a 'girls can be anything' approach, they are described by their female students as contributing to the girls' loss of voice. The girls observe that their teachers appeared to be offering contradictory messages about being autonomous (you can be anything) and being nice.

Being 'nice' has consequences that are personal, social and political. In order to be nice, one sometimes has to 'cover over.' In the previous chapter, for example, we referred to Walkerdine's (1990a) analysis of an episode that she witnessed in an infant classroom. Two boys were acting up and engaging in sex talk banter, referring to one of the girls in the class as 'cunt'. When the teacher, Miss Baxter, tried to shush them, they proceeded to make fun of her name, and taunt her with sexual and bathroom language. Miss Baxter tried to 'normalize', or cover over the activity with a 'boys will be boys' approach. (Mr. Kimble would only have had to blow his whistle once for the boys to fall in line). However, as Walkerdine observes, the boys were not 'just small boys' and the teacher was not 'uniquely a teacher'; she was also a woman:

> In this case the teacher is a woman and while that itself is crucial, it is only because of the ways in which 'woman' signifies that we can understand the specific nature of the struggle. The boys' resistance to her can be understood in terms both of their assertion of their difference from her and their seizing of power through constituting her as the powerless object of sexist discourse. Although they are not physically grown men they can take the positions of men through language, and

in so doing gain power which has material effects. Their power is gained by refusing to be constituted as the powerless objects in her discourse and recasting her as the powerless object of their oppression. Of course, she has not in a sense ceased to signify as one: she has been made to signify as the powerless object of male sexual discourse. (p. 5)

Walkderdine observes that when the boys take on the teacher as 'cunt', she is no longer 'just a teacher' trying to shush them, she is objectified as a woman.

Covering over points to the contradictions and tensions between the surface and deep structures of our everyday life texts. Zannis (1994), in her investigation of feminist pedagogy in her own classroom, offers a revisionist reading of her prior experience of 'we girls can do anything' schooling in the 1980s:

> . . . in my high school, we, as female students, were encouraged to do all that we could. We were told that we could enter any field we wished, and the success of graduates who entered male dominated fields was shared with us on a regular basis. This is important because it did give us the incentive to try hard, to strive for what we wanted. It also initiated many comments which came my way to the effect that it was curious that I 'only wanted to be a teacher' when, in fact, I could do anything. I have only recently come to realize that we were encouraged to go forward, take great strides in the advancement of women, by being as like men as we could in our education. (p. 4)

In the same way that some girls may be embarrassed to admit to playing with Barbie, are some young women embarrassed to admit they 'just' want to be teachers? Are women often encouraged to 'cover over' their desire to do women's work? What does this say about teacher identity and the social images of teaching? And what are the implications for young men who want to become elementary, or even kindergarten teachers? As we noted in chapter 6, it is also important to ask what kinds of struggles and texts men are compelled to live with when they want to be elementary teachers.

We have drawn on a diverse body of literature in order to situate our claim that when the subject of a girls' text such as Barbie, emblematic of young girls' desires and fantasies, takes over a classroom to do women's work, practitioners, teacher educators and cultural theorists should pay attention! We have argued that the deep structure of Barbie is desire, beauty, power, and glamour — features that become highly problematized when the surface structure is such that she is 'dressed to teach'. We have taken this analysis to the elementary school classroom where we have argued that, for female teachers, this same deep structure/surface structure dilemma exists. A similar observation can be found in the work of Walkderine (1990):

The staffroom is full of women eating cheese or grapefruit. Each of them knows about diet and eating and sexuality. They are willing and happy to talk about these, caught inside what they are: the unique combination of worker and woman, dependent and independent, free and trapped (extract from fieldnotes of primary school staffroom). (p. 28)

Our reading of Barbie and other texts of romance has helped illustrate the ways in which the inherent contradictions and widespread devaluing of the popular texts of girls' and women's culture has relevance for a critical reading of 'teacher'. A consideration of the professional identity of teachers is incomplete if it fails to acknowledge the presence and import of the deep structures of gender, romance, and sexuality. In the final chapter, we shift our focus slightly, from a cultural reading of texts such as Arnold Schwarzenegger and Barbie, to a consideration of how such texts might be 'turned inward', to become what we shall term 'the teacher gaze'.

8 Through the Teacher's Gaze

> We need to widen our understanding of how we are taught, and how
> we learn, and how we know, and this involves analyzing the peda-
> gogy of popular culture. (Scholle, 1991, p. 3)

The landscape of schooling and the work of teachers have been and
continue to be important sites in the cultural production of the texts of childhood. In a very real sense television and other forms of popular culture serve
as the first school for young children and as the first Faculty of Education for
adults who wish to become teachers. In the countless classrooms of fiction and
film in which we are all immersed, we are exposed to both right and left wing
images of teaching, image-texts that can be agents of change and subversion,
as well as invisible but powerful agents of reproduction and conservatism.
These teacher images vie for children's attention as they grow up, some of
them to become teachers.

The previous chapters have looked at the multiplicity of these teacher
images from primary, secondary, and tertiary texts and traced some of the
centripetal forces that hold them in proximity so that, collectively and dialectically, they constitute an unnoticed cumulative cultural text called teacher.
How to read this text? How does one best proceed? The line-up of teacher
images that parade up and down the pages of this book is not a straight one.
Moreover, the images weave in and out of focus as a new context or intertext
alters the background or obscures the foreground. Certain images abruptly
crack, as a jarring element fragments their unity. The implausibility of some
images and the juxtaposition of contradictory messages within the same image
problematize our everyday conceptions of teacher. We end up, not with a
sharp composite image of teacher, but with a kaleidoscopic collage of fuchsia
shirts, hairnets and buns, bulging biceps, long shapeless dresses, scowling
faces, sparkling eyes, magic wands, tender smiles. And always, the eternal
chalkdust, pointers, apples, and numbers.

It is not teachers who produce films like *Kindergarten Cop* or *Stand and
Deliver* or *The Prime of Miss Jean Brodie* — nor should it necessarily be. There
is no obvious way to erase images which already exist (McRobbie, 1992); Miss
Brodie, Miss Brooks, Miss Dove, Mr. Chips, Mr. Dadier, Mr. Kimble, Mr. Peepers, Miss Stacy and Mr. Thackeray have become some of society's cliches for
teacher whether teachers like it or not. In one direction, we see anti-heros:

unattractive and asexual, narrow of vision, even malevolent, most of them female. In another direction (or so it seems), we see the heros, the saviours: handsome of figure and face, decisive and bold, but kind, enlightened, liberating, and often male. But what appear to be opposites often merge under the scrutiny of their intertextuality. The hero may be authoritarian (Kindergarten Cop), even fascist (Jean Brodie), an anti-hero cross-dressing as an angel. But what of the vast in-between that links opposing stereotypes? Is that where we construct our professional identities, in the intertexts?

Most of the images of teacher in popular culture are metaphoric. As described in chapter 2, metaphors are two-sided, forcing us to view things differently by linking two images, replacing or 'naming' one with the other. To 'read' metaphors truly, Taylor (1984) implies that it is important to respect their duality, to simultaneously keep both images in mind. This is not always what happens, however, especially as images take on a life of their own, moving away from their historical origins and contexts. As Bowers (1980) warns, the duality often fades, and we focus only on one image, forgetting it represents another. Thus, for example, in *Kindergarten Cop*, we are asked to link and replace the stereotype of kindergarten teacher-as-child-centred-female pedagogue with an image of kindergarten teacher-as-male-action-hero in charge. But is this metaphor credible enough for this linking to occur? After the initial challenge or rupturing, do viewers really leave the theatre with a new perspective, a powerful new image of what kindergarten teachers can be? Or, instead, does the teacher-half of the metaphor fade into the background unattended, ceding its place to the more dominant image of Terminator Schwarzenegger? In viewing the film, are boys and men inclined to identify with 'Kindergarten' or 'Cop'? In chapter 3, we quoted elementary school children who told us that women are particularly suited to teaching because they are nice and not too tough like some men who are perceived as being better suited to high school teaching. Schwarzenegger's role is an attempt to rupture this image, but does anyone notice? And if they do notice, what do they notice? That men-in-charge can do a better job of 'women's work', that police marching drills make for good kindergarten pedagogy? A single convincing reading is problematic.

Similarly, in the comic book episode that features Barbie as a student teacher, it is possible that Barbie-the-fashion-goddess overshadows Barbie-the-teacher. Even if teacher remains in focus, the rupturing that occurs is not necessarily emancipatory. Barbie the teacher is much like many everyday images of good, traditional teachers; she stands in front of the classroom and explains, using audio-visual aids. She is warm compassionate and self-sacrificing, living for and through her students (teaching is not a sideline for her as it is for *Kindergarten Cop*). Projecting themselves in their Barbie doll play, do young girls focus on the fashion and beauty images, preparing themselves for anorexia and plastic surgery as their growing bodies inevitably betray the indelible idealized image they incorporate into their own self-images as women? Perhaps, instead, or also, they identify with the Barbie teacher image, thus becoming socialized into the traditional image of teacher-as-selfless paragon of service, a myth that like so many myths, is rooted in lived reality. Is that where real teacher training begins? Alternatively, perhaps some girls really ARE reading the official ideology of Barbie: girls can do anything, they can be astronauts AND go shopping, they can be teachers AND be sexy and stylish, they don't have to conform to stereotypes, they don't have to turn their backs on women's popular culture in order to walk confidently. In asking these questions, we are searching for the deep or structural metaphors that underlie and often sabotage educational theory and practice, and we are warning against single or simplistic readings, even if they are ideologically appealing to democratic and emancipatory intentions.

From a cultural studies perspective, reading a text closely is in a sense about political incorrectness and the need to 'read wrongly', to misread. In other words, it is often natural and useful to 'get it wrong' in the service of 'getting it right'. Jane Miller (1990) contends that it is the misreadings and the multiple readings, the agreements and the disagreements, that need to be shared in cultural reading. What we propose is also similar to Weiler's (1988) method of 'critical interrogation', where consciousness as well as meaning is questioned, and social life is critically analyzed in conjunction with the text. A critical close reading involves making explicit the dialogue that is implicit in the monologue and reading the world through 'resistant frameworks' (Gilligan, 1991a and 1991b). One way to set up such a framework is to start with the reading perspective of others, something that Harding's (1991) 'standpoint theory' tries to do. Extending Miller's work, we argue that whatever images we wish to avoid, cover up, control, or accommodate are the very ones most likely to be important to situating and reconstructing teacher. As Moss (1989) and Christian-Smith (1990) contend, the general devaluing of popular culture as texts has led to an isolated reading of these texts, so that the readers themselves never have a chance to question the ideologies that link these texts to their social context. Teachers are isolated in their work (Lortie, 1975) and largely unaware of their role in the replication of the cumulative cultural text that they embody.

Seeing Ourselves as Teacher: Cultural Studies, Autobiography and Professional Identity

Fact, fiction, and fantasy mingle together, and instead of trying to work out 'what really happened', I am beginning to see the place of the construction of all those fictions in producing me. But I am fighting back. (Walkerdine, 1990, p. 158)

What to make of images? Our contention is that it is not only *what* we make of images that is important, but also *that* we make something out of them in a critical manner. Popular culture can be a way into ourselves individually and collectively, a stimulus for self-interrogation that can sharpen our professional identities as teachers by providing the contextual, historical, and political background that makes self-interpretation more meaningful and identity more complete. Through multiple readings of our own reactions to teacher images in popular culture, we enter into a dialectical relationship with the polarities, ambiguities, and tensions within the social matrix of teaching. Consequently, interrogating images of teachers in the popular culture of childhood becomes a sort of autobiographical investigation, inevitably involving a deeper sense of the collective identity of teacher as well as some often unexpected insights into one's own individual history and identity. In this final chapter, we turn to the pedagogical significance of cultural studies as a framework for 'a teacher gaze', and illustrate how popular culture may be used as a means of understanding the professional identity of teachers.

> the very notion that our own past experiences may offer some insight into the very ways in which individuals construct themselves into existing relations, thereby themselves reproducing a social formation, itself contains an implicit argument for a particular methodology. (Haug, 1987, p. 34)

In a series of essays, Valerie Walkerdine (1990) describes the use of cultural artefacts such as photographs of herself as a small child to probe her own identity, first as a school girl, and later as a teacher of school girls. In 'Video replay' she turns her gaze inward, using observations of a family watching a movie to examine her own work as a researcher. Her self-study is but an example of the recent work being undertaken by many feminist, life-history, autobiographical, and narrative researchers (for example, Anderson and Jack, 1991; Ayers 1993; Bullough, Knowles and Crow, 1991; Clandinin, 1994; Cole and Knowles, 1994; Goodson, 1994; Grumet, 1988; Pinar, 1980; Raymond, Butt and Townsend, 1992).

Self-study offers an interesting, if challenging, method for reading the cumulative text into which all teachers are born and socialized. By using popular culture itself as a conduit for self-study, it is possible to stir up the sediment of subconscious images that colours intellectual and affective life, bringing to light previously hidden aspects of popular imagery that silently shape personal and collective conceptions of teacher. By directing one's own 'teacher gaze' back and forth from popular images to oneself as teacher, it is possible to conduct a dialectical close reading that includes and situates the individual within the cumulative cultural text. To illustrate, we offer a self-study, a close reading of a teacher educator's reactions to viewing the film *To Sir With Love* (Weber, 1994).

Memorying Against the Text: Popular Culture as Conduit to Self Study

Remembering To Sir With Love : *Emancipatory Filter of the Past?*

Surrounded by a small group of colleagues and graduate students, I settled down comfortably in a darkened university room for a much anticipated trip down memory lane — a screening of *To Sir With Love* — a movie I had seen only once before in my life, more than a quarter of a century ago. As the opening credits rolled, I nodded my head in recognition to the beat of the somewhat hackneyed but effective opening sound-track, remembering fondly the positive impact the film had on me back in the 60s, in what seems to me now to have been another, earlier life. The movie had originally appealed to me on many levels, not the least of which was the basic sex appeal of its star, Sidney Poitier ('teacher as hunk', but that is an anachronism, since adolescent females didn't use the word 'hunk' back then. We said vapid things like 'Isn't he dreamy?' and 'What a dreamboat!'). But I digress, or do I? Is sexuality not an integral part of the images of teachers portrayed in films? Is sex not a basic component of even teachers' lives and identities? As Merleau-Ponty (1962) reminds us, the fundamental aspects of human existence and identity, including human consciousness, are firstly and always embodied. But a human science imbued in the Cartesian dichotomy of mind and body does not take seriously the body or bodily functions in its theoretical deliberations. Irigaray (1990), a French feminist psychoanalyst, points out that all inhabited space is sexuated through our use of body and language, in the way we define the relationship and boundaries of body/other, commanding a space, as in the declarative 'I', or sharing space, as in the more inclusive 'I'.

To return to the movie, I was only two years out of high school myself when I first saw *To Sir With Love*. I remember that I sympathized and empathized with Pamela, the female senior high student who had a rather serious romantic crush on her teacher, Mark Thackeray, otherwise known affectionately as 'Sir'. Like the students in his class, I marvelled at the heady freedom Sir seemed to be offering: Rather than continuing to plod through the boring exercises of the prescribed school curriculum, Sir suggested that they use class time to talk seriously about life. In a dramatic act of rebellion, he flung the school textbooks into the wastebasket, saying 'Those are out. They are useless to you.' Oh, how I wished I had a teacher like Mark Thackeray when I was in high school, someone who recognized the dull, lifeless nature of the official curriculum that was uncaringly and unrelentingly force-fed to us hour after hour, day after day. What Sir seemed to be offering was a new bridge between knowledge and life, between youth and adulthood, between thinking and acting, between working class failure and middle class success. For me, at that time, the movie offered a seductive glimpse of possibilities: schooling as meaningful, as connected with life, work aspirations, even love and romance — subjects much on the mind of adolescent girls.

Other aspects of the film that made a lasting impression on me were what I at the time perceived as positive and just stands on issues of race and class. Sir was a black man from a British colonial working class background of poverty who, by dint of hard work, intelligence, and determination, completed his training as an engineer and strove to succeed in a middle class, white man's world. He conducted himself with dignity, setting a high standard of morality and a good example of middle class language and decorum for his working class students. As one of his students put it, 'Sir, I don't get it. You're like us, you're one of us, but you're not like us.' Both explicitly and tacitly, Sir seemed to be telling his students that education combined with hard work was the way out of poverty and up into the middle class. Unlike Mr. Weston, one of the school's teachers who disparaged the student body as the 'Great London unwashed', Sir genuinely cared for his students. Without preaching to them, he helped them struggle with their own racism and violence, inspiring them to attend the funeral of the mother of the class's only black student, and to reject violence as a childish rather than an adult response to situations of injustice. To my young and rather naive political awareness of the 1960s, the movie seemed to reveal hopeful possibilities of education and teaching as ways towards a more just and harmonious world, something I thought was worth striving for. As Giroux (1993b) might put it, the movie staked out a terrain of hope, offering subject positions from which viewers 'could project an image of themselves as future teachers; an image that encouraged them to identify themselves as agents rather than as mere technicians' (p. 41). It's the sort of film that makes some people 'feel good about themselves as "teachers-in-the-making"' (*ibid*).

I remember identifying with Sir as he battled with cynical teachers, prejudice and ignorance, ultimately rejecting a much more prestigious career as an engineer for the love of teaching, for the love of children. Romantic!? Heady stuff?! Prior to seeing the movie, I had never even considered a career in teaching, but I did not forget that film. It lingered somewhere in the sedimentary collage of images that form the inchoate, primary material for thinking and feeling.

The Disrupting Filter of the Present: Sexism, Power, Oppression?

Watching the movie some twenty-seven years later, I felt transported back in time, once more experiencing Sir's impact as a teacher, person and man. The screening was progressing as anticipated, a rather nostalgic interlude, when in a split second, a scene abruptly and unexpectedly tore into my reveries, shocking me into disbelief, and then rousing me to an anger I felt viscerally, physically.

The scene that so strongly attracted and held my attention occurred as Sir

entered the school and walked up the stairs to his classroom just moments
after some of his male students had tossed a water bomb down out of the
classroom window at him. When Sir entered the classroom, he smelled something burning and saw that someone had set fire to a feminine sanitary napkin
in a metal container. Outraged, Mr. Thackeray ordered all of the boys out of
the classroom without reprimanding them and then turned to the girls who
remained inside. I listened in stunned disbelief as I heard my beloved Sir shout
at his female students:

> I'm sick of your foul language, your crude behaviour, and your slut-
> tish manner. There are certain things that a decent woman keeps
> private, and only a filthy slut would have done this. Those who stood
> by and encouraged her are just as bad. I'm going to leave this room
> for five minutes, and when I return, that DISGUSTING object had
> better be removed and the window opened to clear away the stench.

Sir then ran to the staffroom where he paced back and forth ranting,
frustrated with himself for losing his temper, referring to 'those kids' as 'the
devil incarnate'. Although thus far in the film it was the boys who had been
trying his patience the most, who had been defying him the most, who had
actually been violent, who had slammed doors and desks, and had even hurled
water bombs out the window at him, when Mark Thackeray vented his frustration — when he finally screamed and yelled — it was not at the boys, but
at the girls! And what did he berate them for? For their sex, for the fact that
they were reminding him they were women. He was offended by their very
femaleness, their sexuality. This teacher, who at other moments in the film
advocated politeness and respect, hurled the word 'slut', not once, but four
times at his female students in the course of the movie.

I cannot remember taking offence at this scene in the same way twenty-
seven years ago. I do not think I was even the least bit angry with Sir. Yet the
word 'slut' must have felt, as it does to me today, like a slap in the face. My
hunch is that I felt meek, a little abashed for the girls, maybe even a little
ashamed somehow. If Sir said we were sluts, then we must have been. If he
hit us (figuratively), then we must have deserved it. Perhaps I also identified
with the teacher, maybe I was even a little glad that the teacher was finally
asserting his control, whipping those kids into shape. Like many of the
disempowered, even like Sir who shed the dress and language of his lower
class roots, maybe I turned my back on my own kind, on girls, to feel empowered, to be on the side of the male authority figure. These speculations
trouble me . . . self-study can be like that!

Absorbed by these glimpses into my changing perspectives as the movie
continued, I almost missed the return of gender to centre stage as Sir addressed
his whole class:

> We are now going to discuss general deportment: First the young
> ladies, they must prove they are worthy and appreciative of the

courtesies we are going to show them. No man likes a slut for long
and only the worst kind marries one. And the competition for men on
the outside is rough.

There was no similar speech about boys proving themselves worthy or
appreciative of courtesies extended to them. It was as if respect extended by
females to males were not a courtesy, but a right, the natural order of things.
To the boys, Sir spoke instead of the mind, saying, 'Toughness is a quality of
mind.' For girls, modesty and heterosexuality, pleasing men, were what was
important. For example, Sir asked an attractive female teaching colleague to
give the girls in his class lessons in applying make-up, and commented that
'Some of them'd be very pretty if they knew how to do it.' This episode gives
a literal perspective on the lyrics of the movie's title song (sung by a female
student) which includes the phrase, 'How do you thank someone who's taken
you from crayons to perfume?'!
    The portrayal of how teachers discipline their students in the movie pro-
vides further insight into society's ambivalence towards and the stereotypes
concerning the intricate interweaving of gender, power, and violence. During
a discussion with Sir in the staffroom about her worries, about 'handling' the
school's rowdy students, a beginning female teacher, Gillian, voices her fears
about being a woman in relation to the exercise of her authority and reassures
Mark Thackeray, who also questions his own ability to handle the students,
'It'll be much easier for you . . . (you're a man), I'm a little afraid of them.'
    There it is, right on the table: the implication that men, because of their
size, strength, and their very maleness, are not afraid, and have less difficulty
controlling and maintaining order in a classroom than women do (an implication that those of us who have experienced the forceful power exerted by a
strict female teacher know to be false). But being a large man does not seem
to be enough. When addressing the class, Sir is almost always gripping a thick
stick, often slapping it rhythmically into his hands — first a broken wooden
table leg (perhaps inadvertently providing a model for the boy who later
threatens another teacher with a broken wooden leg), then a thick, rounded
pointer. Pointer as phallus, as weapon? Talk softly and carry a big stick! Over
and over again, the film's verbal, official stance towards non-violence is con-
tradicted by an explicit countertext of action that legitimizes the threats of male
violence and reinforces stereotypes of women as not being naturally suited for
positions of power.

Rebellion As Oppression?

Alerted now to the fact that the movie as I remembered it might not be what
the film would mean to me now, I continued watching with a wary eye, almost
dreading any interpretation that would force me to reevaluate my lifelong
assessment of Sir as a wonderful teacher. But issues of gender, class, race,

sexual orientation and power kept thrusting the movie in an unfavourable light, at least to my teacher educator's eyes of the 1990s.

In the next scene, Sir, calmer now, decides things are going to change in the classroom. Accompanied by a dramatic percussion sound track, there is the scenario I so well remembered, the emphatic thrusting of school books into the wastebasket: an act of defiance, a subversion of the school curriculum, a wake-up call to the students, an invitation to dialogue about things meaningful, a choice of subject matter. Teacher as liberator! Teacher as rebel!

Is this dramatic gesture really emancipatory? Or is it a put-down of working class students, saying, in effect, 'you are so hopeless you are beyond schooling, let's not worry your pretty little heads with book learning'? In his chapter entitled 'Reclaiming the social: Pedagogy, resistance, and politics in celluloid culture', Giroux (1993b) is not impressed with a similar gesture posed by another high school teacher, Mr. Keating, in the more contemporary film, *Dead Poets Society*:

> Resistance demands no sacrifices, no risks, no attempt to deconstruct the relationship between the margins and the centres of power. On the contrary, resistance in Keating's pedagogy serves to depoliticize and decontextualize since it is only developed within a romanticized aesthetic. (p. 44)

Can Giroux's (1993b) condemnation of Mr. Keating's curricular rebellion be applied to Mr. Thackeray? Although Sir takes his students out of the school on 'progressive' class outings, he compliantly follows the school rules and submits to authority, making no fuss when permission for these trips is ultimately withdrawn. Sir takes serious steps to reform the academic lived curriculum in his classroom, but outside of the classroom is a different matter. He closes ranks with the other teachers who are bullying or rude, refusing to publicly entertain any criticism of other teachers from his students. Ultimately, what counts as culture for Sir are the trips to the museums and a socially appropriate use of middle class language and behaviour. Having worked his way up to the middle class, he seems, at times, to be practising a policy of exclusion, telling students they can accomplish anything they set their minds to, ignoring through omission the multitude of social and political impediments these children have to face. The movie's implicit modelling of heterosexuality as the only acceptable orientation, its very explicit reinforcement of gender stereotypes, its 'pull yourselves up by your bootstraps' approach to race and class differences, stamp it with a date, an era, and ultimately, a political orientation that is not as radical in its deep structure as the surface imagery might indicate. And yet, this film WAS disrupting in its effect. It inspired me and countless others to rethink in a critical way what teaching could be, what curriculum could be.

There are also, perhaps, other mitigating perspectives or questions that should not be too quickly ignored. Who can authoritatively label a group to be 'oppressed' or 'emancipated'? Many of the children's parents are very pleased with Sir's attempts to interest their children in what could be labelled middle-class Western High Culture and Education. Their reaction reminds me of a conversation that I overheard in an African country struggling to come to terms with its post-colonial status. A woman was berating an official who was suggesting that they completely abandon the British curriculum and system of education: 'Do you think our children don't deserve a Western education? Are you saying we should provide a local education that won't stand up in the international arena of competition?' There does not seem to be an easy answer or indeed a single answer. There does seem to be a need for continuing dialogue and reflection, and for a multitude of voices. We need to listen not only to our own critical voices, but also to people like Sir, himself from a working class, black background, and also, to those who come from the same background as Sir but do not share his views. It is the dialectic between these multiple readings that has emancipatory and democratic potential.

Re-imaging Teacher

What is apparent by now is how quickly I picked up on issues that were invisible to me twenty-seven years ago; issues of power, class, race, and most especially, gender. My reactions to reviewing this film inadvertently exposed certain political and cultural elements of my personal experience. A child of the fifties, I reacted to violence and male authority like many other females did and still do — submissively, meekly. Similarly, I was imbued with Romantic notions concerning equality of race and class, notions that were tinged with a white, colonial, middle-class wash that is so old and faded and translucent, I didn't notice it on my skin, mistakenly assuming it had washed off long ago. In the sixties, I was not as attuned to the implications of our propensity to dichotomize each other in terms of gender, class, race, age, and ethnicity in the same way that I am today, a realization that sheds light not only on my personal development, but on the social context of the 60s in North America.

> Those who use a discourse of 'the pinks and the blues' continually searching for contrastive differences, may assume that girls and boys sharply divide as two separate and unitary types of beings. But the social world is not that simple. There are many ways of being a boy or girl, some of them overlapping, some varying by context, some shifting along lines of race, ethnicity, class, and age. (Thorne, 1993, p. 158)

The experience of self-study through revisiting important popular culture texts can be humbling and transformative. It serves as a reminder of the importance of the reading of the text to a text's emancipatory potential. Had I not been inspired by the emancipatory possibilities of teaching in what I now consider a misreading of the movie, would I have arrived as surely to my

137

current more critical perspective? As an educator, this experience of self-study inclines me to be more open and less judgmental about the reactions of my students to films such as *Dead Poets Society*. Conservatism and revolution are so often two sides of the same coin (Marcel, 1978).

Self-study reveals not only the individual and idiosyncratic elements of experience, but also the pervasive influences of the culture of the social group in which we are raised. Revolutionary messages can be wrapped in conservative packaging, while calls to preserve the status quo slip unobtrusively into exhortations for change. Personal conceptions of teaching are seldom coherent and unequivocal, reflecting the contradictory and ambivalent stances that pervade the popular culture of teaching. Misreading is inevitable and even helpful, especially when it is brought to consciousness and is one of a series of multiple readings. If I view the film ten years from now, will I spot with embarrassment some type of glass cage that imprisons me even now? Will it be the confinement of Cultural Studies that chafes?

The importance of self-study is illustrated by Weiler's (1988) observation, in her study of memory, that female teachers often gloss over the details of their lives, 'forgetting', for example, that they were forced to go out to work to support members of the family, and 'remembering' instead that they had 'always had a calling to teach', evidence to the contrary. There are struggles that we need to remember: The violence in classrooms, the power that is blatantly abused, the sexual innuendoes, the racism, the harrassment, the angst that we feel when we must fail a student or when a student confides in us something we would rather not know. Is there a reluctance to interrogate images, to read the cumulative cultural text? Why do we not want to confer visibility on the classroom, our classrooms, as sites of struggle? — because we feel that we are weak, that it is not academic, that we should be 'over that'?

Self-study, autobiography, and life history are too easily dismissed out of hand as egocentric and self-indulgent. A few people publish their stories, and the faddist tendency in educational research gets restless: 'We've done that, time to move on to the next fad, the next image.' Our contention is that research, including self-study, should indeed be dismissed if it is done or written in such a way that shuts out the reader, closes down dialogue, or ignores the intertextual nature of all research. Done dialectically and critically, however, we argue that these approaches constitute a valuable acknowledgment that we are, after all, 'readers in history, readers with a history' (Miller, 1990), and offer meaningful ways of simultaneously interrogating the personal and the social, providing insight into the general (cumulative text) while focusing on the particular.

In 1984, I wrote what for me was one of the most painful essays of my life. 'Dreams from an ordinary childhood' was a 'coming out' as working-class, a realization that for years I had been frightened to reveal my past in academic circles and had engaged in a kind of masquerade in which I had not only felt ashamed of my background,

but had come to the Left and to feminism entirely through academia
. . . I found no space to address the formation of my own subjectivity,
a working-class girl who became a teacher and then an academic
. . . Just as it is argued that there is not one black struggle but many
black struggles, so the struggles of class are many, varied and full
of contradictions . . . In recent years, while gender and race have
become common currency, it has become almost impossible to speak
about class . . . I call myself an 'educated working-class woman' . . .
This may be a fictional identity like all the others, but it allows something to be spoken and some things to come together: educated,
working-class, and woman — three terms which I thought were
hopelessly fragmented. (Walkerdine, 1990, pp. 157–8)

Our suggestion is that teachers appropriate the tools and approaches of
cultural studies for their own project. As we note in chapter 1, because it
focuses on popular culture, cultural studies is necessarily about interrogating
inclusion and exclusion. Why are some texts and images excluded from school
and from our deliberations about schooling? What makes some texts canonized and others popular? A cultural studies framework focuses on those texts
which are on the 'wrong side of the track'. We propose that schooling and the
work of teachers ought to be interrogated more often within such a framework, but caution that these interrogations or readings are limited in value if
they are restricted to a simple content analysis which looks only at 'messages'
contained within popular texts. Similarly, it is too simplistic to merely trash
much of popular culture or, alternatively, to romanticize it in an unproblematized
way.

Educators, as cultural theorists, are beginning to map out the dialectics of
multiple readings against and with the popular texts of teaching. Reading these
texts contributes to an awareness of personal professional identity and its
relation to the cumulative cultural text of teacher by highlighting the social
positioning of individual action. A fluid and contextual approach softens and
even dissolves the rigidity of the polarities and false dichotomies that oversimplify the meaning of human experience, enabling us to see the underlying
complementarity of certain surface contradictions. Through dialectic interaction with a text, a close reading changes the reader, sometimes in an empowering manner that can precipitate action by revealing new possibilities or a
more focused vision.

Critical interrogations of the popular images of teaching may lead in surprising directions. For one, we may discover images of hope that please in the
most unlikely of places. For example, it may be that substitute teacher, Starlight, a cartoon Pony, embodies a counter-pedagogy that some teachers might
find emancipatory because it suggests they can be teacher AND 'be themselves'. Barrie Thorne (1993) holds fast to the image of Hansel and Gretel, of
brother and sister, as a concrete image that can hold the abstraction of gender
equality and mutuality. She suggests that examining sources of resistance and

opposition can point the way to alternative arrangements based on equality and mutuality. By clarifying and displaying those images that we do like, by articulating and sharing those that resonate deeply, we breathe new life into them, and their power increases. The project that grows out of a close reading is to imagine and realize other possibilities, ways to get beneath the stereotypes, sometimes, paradoxically, by embracing them. The post-reading project becomes a writing project, one that creates new images, that offers 'a more complex understanding of the dynamics of gender, of tensions and contradictions, and of the hopeful moments that lie within present arrangements' (Thorne, 1993, p. 173), that can help broaden our sense of the possible and give new meaning to the expression, 'That's funny, . . .'

References

ACKER, S. (1992) 'Creating careers: Women teachers at work', *Curriculum Inquiry*, 22(2), pp. 141–163.

ADLER, L.L. (1982) 'Children's drawings as an indicator of individual preferences reflecting group values: A programmatic study', in ADLER, L.L. (Ed) *Cross-Cultural Research at Issue*, New York, Academic Press, pp. 71–98.

AITKEN, J. (1990) 'An education in Romanticism for our time', in WILLINSKY, J. (Ed) *The Educational Legacy of Romanticism*, Waterloo, Ontario, Wilfrid Laurier University Press, pp. 211–30.

ALLAN, J. (1993) 'Male elementary teachers: Experiences and perspectives', in WILLIAMS, C.L. (Ed) *Doing 'Women's Work': Men in Nontraditional Occupations*, Newbury Park, Sage, pp. 113–27.

ALLEN, R. (Ed) (1987) *Channels of Discourse: Television and Contemporary Criticism*, Chapel Hill, North Carolina, University of North Carolina Press.

ANDERSON, K. and JACK, D.C. (1991) 'Learning to listen: Interview techniques and analyses', in GLUCK, S.B. and PATAI, D. (Eds) *Women's Words: The Feminist Practice of Oral History*, New York, Routledge, pp. 11–26.

ANDERSON, R.C. (1977) 'The notion of schemata and the educational enterprise: General discussion of conference', in ANDERSON, R.C., SPIRO, R.J. and MONTAGUE, W.E. (Eds) *Schooling and the Acquisition of Knowledge*, Hillsdale, NJ, Lawrence Erlbaum Associates, pp. 415–31.

ARMALINE, W. and HOOVER, R. (1989) 'Field experience as a vehicle for transformation: Ideology, education and reflective practice', *Journal of Teacher Education*, 40(2), pp. 42–48.

ASKEW, S. and ROSS, C. (1988) *Boys Don't Cry: Boys and Sexism in Education*, Buckingham, Open University Press.

AUCHMUTY, R. (1992) *A World of Girls*, London, The Women's Press.

AYERS, W. (1993) *To Teach — The Journey of a Teacher*, New York, Teachers College Press.

BAKHTIN, M.M. (1986) *The Dialogic Imagination*, EMERSON, C. and HOLQUIST, M. (Trans), Austin, University of Texas Press.

BANDMAN, B. (1967) *The Place of Reason in Education*, Columbus, OH, The Ohio State University Press.

BARBIE FASHION (1992) *The Art of Teaching*, 1(23), pp. 2–15, Nov.

BARTHES, R. (1967) *Elements of Semiology*, LAVERS, A. and SMITH, C. (Trans) London, Jonathan Cape, (Original work published 1964).

References

BERGER, P. and PULLBERG, S. (1964) 'Reification and the sociological critique of consciousness', *History and Theory*, 4.

BEST, R. (1983) *We've All Got Scars: What Boys and Girls Learn in Elementary School*, Bloomington, Indiana Press.

BIKLEN, S.K. (1994) *Imagining Teachers: Gender, Race and Identity in the 1950s*. Paper presented at the Annual Meeting of the American Education Research Association, New Orleans, April.

BOGATYREV, P.G. (1971) *The Function of Folk Costume in Moravian Slovkia*, (Trans) CRUN, R.G. Approaches to Semiotics 5, The Hague, Mouton.

BOOTH, D. (Ed) (1993) *Dr. Knickerbocker and Other Rhymes: A Canadian Collection*, Toronto, Kids Can Press.

BOWERS, C.A. (1980) 'Curriculum as cultural reproduction: An examination of metaphor as a carrier of ideology', *Teachers College Record*, 82, pp. 267–89.

BRITZMAN, D.P. (1986) 'Cultural myths in the making of a teacher: Biography and social structure in teacher education', *Harvard Educational Review*, 56(4), pp. 442–56.

BRITZMAN, D.P. (1991) *Practice Makes Practice: A Critical Study of Learning to Teach*, Albany, NY, State University of New York Press.

BRITZMAN, D.P. (1992) 'The terrible problem of knowing thyself: Toward a poststructural account of teacher identity', *Journal of Curriculum Theorizing*, 9(3), pp. 23–46.

BROWN, L.M. and GILLIGAN, C. (1992) *Meeting at the Crossroads: Women's Psychology and Girls' Development*, Cambridge, MA, Harvard University Press.

BROWN, R.H. (1978) *A Poetic for Sociology*, Cambridge, Cambridge University Press.

BRUNNER, D.D. (1991) *Stories of Schooling in Films and Television: A Cultural Studies Approach to Teacher Education*. Paper presented at the Annual Meeting of the American Educational Research Association, Chicago, April.

BUCHLER, J. (1955) *Nature and Judgement*, New York, Columbia University Press.

BULLOUGH, R.V. (1991) 'Exploring personal teaching metaphors in preservice teacher education', *Journal of Teacher Education*, 42(1), pp. 43–51.

BULLOUGH, R.V. Jr., KNOWLES, J.G. and CROW, N.A. (1991) *Emerging as a Teacher*, New York, Routledge.

BURGIN, V. (1986) *The End of Art Theory: Criticism and Post-Modernity*, Atlantic Highlands, New Jersey, Humanities Press International.

BYARS, J. (1991) *All that Hollywood Allows: Re-reading Gender in 1950s Melodrama*, Chapel Hill, University of North Carolina Press.

CADOGAN, M. and CRAIG, P. (1986) *You're a Brick Angela!: The Girls' Story 1839–1985*, London, Victor Gollancz.

CALDERHEAD, J. and ROBSON, M. (1991) 'Images of teaching: Student teachers' early conceptions of classroom practice', *Teaching and Teacher Education*, 7(1), pp. 1–8.

CAMPBELL, N. and MOORE, M. (1969) *Learn Ev'rything (From Anne of Green*

Gables), London, Chappell & Co. Copyright by Norman Campbell and Donald Harron, Avonlea Music.

CAPRIO, B. (1992) *The Mystery of Nancy Drew: Girl Sleuth on the Couch*, Trabuco Canyon, CA, Source Books.

CHAMPION, R.H. (1984) 'Faculty reported use of research in teacher preparation course: Six instructional scenarios', *Journal of Teacher Education*, 35(5), pp. 9–12.

CHRISTIAN-SMITH, L. (1990) *Becoming a Woman Through Romance*, New York, Routledge.

CHRISTIAN-SMITH, L. (Ed) (1993) *Texts of Desire: Essays on Fiction, Femininity and Schooling*, London, Falmer Press.

CLANDININ, J. (1994) *Biographical Research and Teacher Education*. Paper presented at the Annual Meeting of the American Educational Research Association, New Orleans, April.

CLEARY, B. (1968) *Ramona the Pest*, New York, Avon Books.

CLYDE, J.A. (1994) 'Lessons from Douglas: Expanding our visions of what it means to "know"', *Language Arts*, 71(1), pp. 22–33.

COLE, A. and KNOWLES, J.G. (1994) *Through Preservice Teachers' Eyes: Exploring Field Experiences Through Narrative and Inquiry*, New York, MacMillan.

COLE, A. and KNOWLES, J.G. (1993) *University Supervisors and Preservice Teachers: Clarifying Roles and Negotiating Relationships*. Paper presented at the Annual Conference of the Canadian Society for the Study of Education, Ottawa, Ontario, June.

CONNELL, R.W. (1989) 'Cool guys, swots and wimps: The interplay of masculinity and education', *Oxford Review of Education*, 15(3), pp. 291–303.

CONNELLY, F.M. and CLANDININ, D.J. (1990) 'Stories of experience and narrative inquiry', *Educational Researcher*, 19(4), pp. 2–14.

CONNELLY, F.M. and CLANDININ, D.J. (1985) 'Personal practical knowledge and the modes of knowing: Relevance for teaching and learning', in EISNER, E. (Ed) *Learning and Teaching the Ways of Knowing, 84th Yearbook of the National Society for the Study of Education*, Chicago, University of Chicago Press, pp. 174–98.

CONNELLY, F.M. and CLANDININ, D.J. (1988) *Teachers as Curriculum Planners: Narratives of Experience*, Toronto, OISE Press.

CORLISS, R. (1990) 'Box-office brawn', *Time*, Dec. 24, pp. 52–55.

CORNBLETH, C. (1987) 'The persistence of myth in teacher education and teaching', in POPKEWITZ, T. (Ed) *Critical Studies in Teacher Education: Its Folklore, Theory and Practice*, London, Falmer Press, pp. 186–210.

COULTER, R.P. and McNAY, M. (1993) 'Exploring men's experiences as elementary school teachers', *Canadian Journal of Education*, 18(4), pp. 398–413.

CRAIG, P. (1994) *Oxford Book of Schooldays*, Oxford, Oxford University Press.

CRUME, M. (1988) Images of teachers in novels and films for the adolescent, 1980–1987. (Doctoral dissertation, University of Florida). *Dissertation Abstracts International*, 50, 138A.

DAVIES, B. (1989) *Frogs and Snails and Feminist Tales: Preschool Children and Gender*, North Sydney, Allen & Unwin.

DAY, C. (1990) *Insights into Teachers' Thinking and Practice*, London, Falmer Press.

DE CASTELL, S. (1988) 'Metaphors into models: The teacher as strategist', in HOLBORN, P., WIDEEN, M. and ANDREWS, I. (Eds) *Becoming a Teacher*, Toronto, Kagan and Woo Ltd, pp. 64–83.

DEANE, P. (1991) *Mirrors of American Culture: Children's Fiction Series in the Twentieth Century*, Metuchen, New Jersey, The Scarecrow Press.

DELAMONT, S. (1987) 'The primary teacher 1945–1990: Myths and realities', in DELAMONT, S. (Ed) *The Primary School Teacher*, London, Falmer Press, pp. 3–17.

DENNIS, W. (1966) *Group Values Through Children's Drawings*, New York, Wiley.

DENNIS, W. (1970) 'Good enough scores, art experience and modernization', in AL-ISSA, I. and DENNIS, W. (Eds) *Cross-Cultural Studies of Behavior*, New York, Holt, Rinehart & Winston, pp. 134–52.

DENSCOMBE, M. (1982) 'The hidden pedagogy and its implications for teacher training', *British Journal of Sociology of Education*, 3, pp. 249–265.

DERRIDA, J. (1980) *La loi du genre [The law of genre]*, (Trans) RONNELL, A. *Glyph*, 7, pp. 202–32.

DICKMEYER, N. (1989) 'Metaphor, model, and theory in education research', *Teachers College Record*, 91(2), pp. 151–160.

DYER, R. (1985) 'Entertainment and utopia', in NICHOLS, B. (Ed) *Movies and Methods*, Vol. 2. Berkeley, CA, University of California Press.

DYSON, A.H. (1989) *Multiple Worlds of Child Writers*, New York, Teachers College Press.

EFRON, S. and JOSEPH, P.B. (1994) 'Reflections in a mirror — Teacher-generated metaphors from self and others', in JOSEPH, P.B. and BURNAFORD, G.E. (Eds) *Images of Schoolteachers in Twentieth-Century America — Paragons, Polarities, Complexities*, New York, St. Martin's Press, pp. 54–77.

ELBAZ, F. (1991) 'Research on teacher's knowledge: The evolution of a discourse', *Journal of Curriculum Studies*, 23(1), pp. 1–19.

ERAUT, M. (1985) 'Knowledge creation and knowledge use in professional contexts', *Studies in Higher Education*, 10, pp. 117–133.

EVERHART, R. (1983) *Reading, Writing and Resistance*, New York, Routledge & Kegan Paul.

FARBER, P., PROVENZO, E. Jr. and HOLM, G. (Eds) (1994) *Schooling in the Light of Popular Culture*, Albany, NJ, SUNY Press.

FARRAN, D. (1990) 'Analysing a photograph of Marilyn Monroe', in STANLEY, L. (Ed) *Feminist Praxis: Research, Theory and Epistemology in Feminist Sociology*, London, Routledge, pp. 262–73.

FINE, M. (1989) 'Silencing and nurturing voice in an improbable context: Urban adolescents in public school', in GIROUX, H.A. and MCLAREN, P.L. (Eds) *Critical Pedagogy, The State and Cultural Struggle*, (pp. 152–173), Albany, NY, SUNY Press, pp. 152–73.

FISCHER, J.C. and KIEFER, A. (1994) 'Constructing and discovering images of your teaching', in JOSEPH, P.B. and BURNAFORD, G.E. (Eds) *Images of Schoolteachers in Twentieth-Century America — Paragons, Polarities, Complexities*, New York, St. Martin's Press, pp. 29–53.

FISKE, J. (1987a) *Television Culture*, London, Methuen.

FISKE, J. (1987b) 'British cultural studies and television', in ALLEN, R. (Ed) *Channels of Discourse*, London, Methuen, pp. 254–89.

FISKE, J. (1989) *Understanding Popular Culture*, Boston, Unwin Hyman.

FOFF, A. (1956) *The Teacher As Hero*, in FOFF, A. and GRAMBS, J. (Eds) *Reading in Education*, New York, Harpers, p. 21.

FREEMAN, G. (1976) *The Schoolgirl Ethic: The Life and Work of Angela Brazil*, London, Allen Lane.

FRITH, G. (1987) '"The time of your life": The meaning of the school story', in WEINER, G. and ARNOT, M. (Eds) *Gender Under Scrutiny*, London, The Open University, pp. 117–33.

GADAMER, H-G. (1975) *Truth and Method*, (Trans) BARDEN, G. and CUMMING, J. New York, Crossroad, (Original work published 1960).

GAMMAN, L. and MARSHMENT, M. (Eds) (1989) *The Female Gaze: Women as Viewers of Popular Culture*, Seattle, Washington, The Real Comet Press.

GARRETT, A. and McCUE, H.P. (Eds) (1989) *Authors and Artists for Young Adults*, Detroit, MI, Gale Research.

GASKELL, J. and McLAREN, A. (1987) *Women and Education: A Canadian Perspective*, Calgary, Detselig.

GATHORNE-HARDY, J. (1977) *The Public School Phenomenon, 597–1977*, London, Hodder and Stoughton.

GERBNER, G. (1963) 'Smaller than life: Teachers and schools in the mass media', *Phi Delta Kappan*, 44, pp. 202–5.

GIDDENS, A. (1991) *Modernity and Self-identity: Self and Society in the Late Modern Age*, Stanford, CA, Stanford University Press.

GILBERT, P. and TAYLOR, S. (1991) *Fashioning the Feminine: Girls, Popular Culture and Schooling*, North Sydney, Allen and Unwin.

GILLIGAN, C. (1991b) 'Joining the resistance: Psychology, politics, and women', *Michigan Quarterly Review*, 29(4), pp. 501–36.

GILLIGAN, C. (1991a) *Women, Girls and Psychotherapy: Reframing Resistance*, New York, The Haworth Press.

GILMAN, S.L. (1985) *Difference and Pathology: Stereotypes of Sexuality, Race, and Madness*, Ithaca, New York, Cornell University Press.

GIROUX, H.A. (1981) *Ideology, Culture, and the Process of Schooling*, Philadelphia, Temple University Press.

GIROUX, H.A. (1993a) *Living Dangerously: Multiculturalism and the Politics of Difference*, New York, Peter Lang.

GIROUX, H.A. (1993b) 'Reclaiming the social: Pedagogy, resistance, and politics in celluloid culture', in COLLINS, J., RADNER, H. and COLLINS, A.P. (Eds) *Film Theory Goes to The Movies*, New York, Routledge, pp. 37–55.

References

Giroux, H.A. and Simon, R. (1989a) *Popular Culture, Schooling, and Everyday Life*, Toronto, OISE Press.

Giroux, H.A. and Simon, R. (1989b) 'Schooling, popular culture, and a pedagogy of possibility', in Giroux, H. and Simon, R. (Eds) *Popular Culture, Schooling and Everyday Life*, Toronto, OISE Press, pp. 219–35.

Goffman, E. (1959) *The Presentation of Self in Everyday Life*, New York, Doubleday Anchor Books.

Goldberg, M. (1992) 'Expressing and assessing understanding through the arts', *Phi Delta Kappan*, 73(8), pp. 619–23.

Goodlad, J.I. (1984) *A Place Called School*, New York, McGraw-Hill.

Goodman, J. and Kelly, T. (1988) 'Out of the mainstream: Issues confronting the male profeminist elementary school teacher', *Interchange*, 19(2), pp. 1–14.

Goodson, I.F. (1980) 'Life histories and the study of schooling', *Interchange*, 11(4), pp. 62–77.

Goodson, I.F. (1994) 'Studying the teacher's life and work', *Teaching and Teacher Education*, 10(1), pp. 29–37.

Goodson, I. and Walker, R. (Eds) (1991) *Biography, Identity, & Schooling*, London, Falmer Press.

Grant, G. (1992) 'The sources of structural metaphors in teacher knowledge: Three cases', *Teaching and Teacher Education*, 8(5/6), pp. 433–40.

Grossberg, L., Nelson, C. and Treichler, P. (1992) *Cultural Studies*, New York, Routledge.

Grugeon, E. (1993) 'Gender implications of children's playground culture', in Woods, P. and Hammersley, M. (Eds) *Gender and Ethnicity in Schools: Ethnographic Accounts*, London, Routledge, pp. 11–33.

Grumet, M. (1988) *Bitter Milk: Women and Teaching*, Amherst, University of Massachusetts Press.

Grumet, M. (1981) 'Pedagogy for patriarchy: The feminization of teaching', *Interchange*, 12, pp. 165–84.

Harding, S. (1991) *Whose Science? Whose Knowledge? Thinking from Women's Lives*, Ithaca, NY, Cornell University Press.

Hargreaves, A. and Fullan, M.G. (Eds) (1992) *Understanding Teacher Development*, New York, Teachers College Press.

Haug, F. (1987) (Ed) *Female Sexualization: A Collective Work of Memory*, (Trans) Carter, E. London, Verso.

Hawkes, T. (1972) *Metaphor*, London, Methuen.

Holm, G. (1994) 'Learning in style: The portrayal of schooling in Seventeen magazine', in Farber, P., Provenzo, E. Jr. and Holm, G. (Eds) *Schooling in the Light of Popular Culture*, Albany, NY, SUNY Press, pp. 59–80.

Hunt, D. (1987) *Beginning with Ourselves: In Practice, Theory, and Human Affairs*, Cambridge, MA, Brookline.

Hunter, E. (1984) *The Blackboard Jungle*, New York, Arbor House. (Original work published 1953).

Hutcheon, L. (1989) *The Politics of Postmodernism*, New York, Routledge.

IRIGARAY, L. (1993) *Je, Tu, Nous: Toward a Culture of Difference*, (Trans) MARTIN, A. New York, Routledge.

JOHNSTON, S. (1992) 'Images: A way of understanding the practical knowledge of student teachers', *Teaching & Teacher Education*, 8(2), pp. 123–36.

JONES, G. (1991) *Crocus Hill Notebook*, London, Ontario, The Althouse Press.

JOSEPH, P.B. and BURNAFORD, G.E. (1994a) 'Contemplating images of school-teachers in American culture', in JOSEPH, P.B. and BURNAFORD, G.E. (Eds) *Images of Schoolteachers in Twentieth-Century America — Paragons, Polarities, Complexities*, New York, St. Martin's Press, pp. 3–25.

JOSEPH, P.B. and BURNAFORD, G.E. (Eds) (1994b) *Images of Schoolteachers in Twentieth-Century America — Paragons, Polarities, Complexities*, New York, St. Martin's Press.

KEENE, C. (1986) *The Nancy Drew Files: Secrets Can Kill*, New York, Pocket Books.

KERMODE, M. (1991) 'Kindergarten Cop', (Review), *Monthly Film Bulletin*, 58(685), pp. 47–8.

KINDER, M. (1991) *Playing with Power in Movies, Television, and Video Games: From Muppet Babies to Teenage Mutant Ninja Turtles*, Berkeley, CA, University of California Press.

KLEIN, T. (1988) 'Arnold Schwarzenegger: More than muscles', *The Saturday Evening Post*, March, pp. 41–4.

KOPPITZ, E.M. (1984) *Psychological Evaluation of Human Figure Drawings by Middle School Pupils*, New York, Grune & Stratton.

KOWINSKI, W.S. (1985) *The Malling of America: An Inside Look At The Great Consumer Paradise*, New York, William Morrow & Co.

LACEY, C. (1977) *The Socialization of Teachers*, London, Methuen.

LAKOFF, G. and JOHNSON, M. (1980) *Metaphors We Live by*, Chicago, University of Chicago Press.

LANGER, S. (1971) 'The cultural importance of the Arts', in SMITH, R.A. (Ed) *Aesthetics and Problems of Education*, Chicago, University of Illinois Press, pp. 86–96.

LAVER, J. (1949) *Style in Costume*, London, Oxford University Press.

LAWTON, D. (1984) 'Metaphor and the curriculum', in TAYLOR, W. (Ed) *Metaphors of Education*, London, Heinemann Educational Books, pp. 79–88.

LEPMAN, J. (Ed) (1971) *How Children See Our World*, New York, Avon Books.

LÉVI-STRAUSS, C. (1963) *Structural Anthropology*, (Trans) JACOBSON, C. and GRUNDFEST SCHOEPF, B., New York, Basic Books.

LIPSITZ, G. (1990) *Time Passages: Collective Memory and American Popular Culture*, Minneapolis, University of Minnesota Press.

LISTON, D.P. and ZEICHNER, K.N. (1991) *Teacher Education and The Social Conditions of Schooling*, London, Routledge.

LORTIE, D. (1975) *School Teacher: A Sociological Study*, Chicago, IL, University of Chicago Press.

LOWENFELD, V. and BRITTAIN, W.L. (1975) *Creative and Mental Growth*, London, Macmillan Co.

LURIE, A. (1990) *Don't Tell The Grown-Ups: Why Kids Love The Books They Do*, London, Avon.

LURIE, A. (1981) *The Language of Clothes*, New York, Random House.

LUTTRELL, W. (1993) 'The teachers, they all had their pets: Concepts of gender, knowledge and power', *Signs, Journal of Women in Culture and society*, 18(3), pp. 505–46.

MARCEL, G. (1978) *Homo Viator: Introduction to a Metaphysic of Hope*, London, Peter Smith Publishing.

MARTIN, A.M. (1988) *The Baby-Sitters Club*, New York, Scholastics.

MASON, B.A. (1975) *The Girl Sleuth: A Feminist Guide*, New York, Feminist Press.

MCNIFF, K.K. (1981) Sex differences in children's art. Doctoral dissertation. Boston University, School of Education.

MCROBBIE, A. (1991) *Feminism and Youth Culture*, Cambridge, MA, Unwin Hyman.

MCROBBIE, A. (1992) 'Post-Marxism and cultural studies: A post-script', in GROSSBERG, L., NELSON, C. and TREICHLER, P. *Cultural Studies*, New York, Routledge, pp. 719–30.

MEAD, M. (1962) *The School in American Culture*, Cambridge, MA, Harvard University Press. (Original work published 1951).

MERLEAU-PONTY, M. (1962) *Phenomenology of Perception*, (Trans) SMITH, C. London, Routledge & Kegan Paul.

MILLER, C. (1994) 'Notes', *Seventeen*, August, 12.

MILLER, J. (1990) *Seductions: Studies in Reading and Culture*, Cambridge, MA, Harvard University Press.

MILLER, J. (1992) *More Has Meant Women: The Feminization of Schooling*, London, The Tafnell Press.

MILLER, S.I. and FREDERICKS, M. (1988) 'Uses of metaphor: A qualitative case study', *Qualitative Studies in Education*, 1(3), pp. 263–72.

MITCHELL, C.A. (1982) 'I only read novels and that sort of thing. Exploring the aesthetic response', *English Quarterly*, Summer, pp. 67–77.

MITCHELL, C.A., MOONILAL-MASUR, P. and CINCIK, E. (1992) 'Dear diary: Exploring gender and genre in the writing-to-learn classroom', *English Quarterly*, 24(2).

MITCHELL, C.A. and REID-WALSH, J. (in press-a) 'And I want to thank you Barbie: Barbie as a site for cultural interrogation', *Review of Education/ Pedagogy/ Culture*.

MITCHELL, C.A. and REID-WALSH, J. (in press-b) *The Juvenile Mystery Series: The Case of Nancy Drew and the Hardy Boys*, New York, Twayne Publishing.

MITCHELL, C.A. and REID-WALSH, J. (1994) *The Case of the Serious Series Reader: The Cumulative Cultural Text*. Paper presented at the Annual Conference of the Association of Bibliotherapy of Canada, Calgary, Alberta, June.

MITCHELL, C.A. and WEBER, S.J. (1993) *Where Are You, Mr. Schwarzenegger? Images of Teaching in the Popular Culture of Childhood*. Children's Popular Culture Conference, New Orleans, April.

MONTGOMERY, L.M. (1942) *Ann of Avonlea*, Toronto, Ryerson. (First published 1909).

MORITZ, C. (Ed) (1991) *Current Biography Yearbook — 1991*, New York, The H.W. Wilson Company.

MOSS, G. (1989) *Un/popular Fictions*, London, University of London Press.

MULVEY, L. (1975) 'Visual pleasure and narrative cinema', *Screen*, 16(3), pp. 6–18.

MUNBY, H. (1986) 'Metaphor in the thinking of teachers: An exploratory study', *Journal of Curriculum Studies*, 18(2), pp. 197–209.

MUSGRAVE, P.W. (1985) *From Brown to Bunter: The Life and Death of the School Story*, London, Routledge and Kegan Paul.

NELSON, M.K. (1992) 'Using oral histories to reconstruct the experiences of women teachers in Vermont, 1900–50', in GOODSON, I.F. (Ed) *Studying Teachers' Lives*, London, Falmer Press, pp. 167–86.

OPIE, I. (1993) *The People in the Playground*, Oxford, New York, Oxford University Press.

ORAM, A. (1989) 'Embittered, sexless or homosexual: Attacks on spinster teachers 1918–39', in LESBIAN HISTORY GROUP (Eds) *Not a Passing Phase: Reclaiming Lesbians in History 1840–1985*, London, The Women's Press, pp. 99–118.

PAYNE, C. (1984) *Getting What We Ask For*, Westport, CT, Greenwood Press.

PEABODY, R. and EBERSOLE, L. (1993) *Mondo Barbie: An Anthology of Fiction and Poetry*, New York, St. Martin's Press.

PEARSON, A.T. and ROOKE, P.T. (1993) 'Gender studies and teacher education: A proposal', *Canadian Journal of Education*, 18(4), pp. 414–28.

PENELOPE, J. (1990) *Speaking Freely: Unlearning the Lies of the Fathers' Tongues*, New York, Pergamon Press.

PINAR, W. (1980) 'Life history and educational experience: Parts I and II', *Curriculum Theorizing*, 2(2), pp. 59–212; 3(1), pp. 259–86.

POLAN, D. (1993) 'Professors. Discourse', *A Journal of Theoretical Studies in Media and Culture*, 16(1), pp. 28–49.

PROVENZO, E.F. Jr. (1991) *Video Kids: Making Sense of Nintendo*, Cambridge, Harvard University Press.

PROVENZO, E.F., Jr., MCCLOSKEY, G.N., KOTTKAMP, R.B. and COHN, M.M. (1989) 'Metaphor and meaning in the language of teachers', *Teachers College Record*, 90(4), pp. 551–73.

QUIGLY, I. (1982) *The Heirs of Tom Brown's School Days: The English School Story*, London, Chatto and Windus.

RAYMOND, D., BUTT, R. and TOWNSEND, D. (1992) 'Contexts for teacher development: Insights from teachers' stories', in HARGREAVES, A. and FULLAN, M.G. (Eds) *Understanding Teacher Development*, New York, Teachers College Press, pp. 143–61.

REID-WALSH, J. and MITCHELL, C. (1993) *Nancy Drew: The Girl Who Can Do Everything*. Paper presented at the Annual Conference of the Canadian Women's Studies Association, Ottawa, Ontario, June.

REYNOLDS, K. (1990) *Girls Only? Gender and Popular Children's Fiction in Britain, 1880–1910*, Philadelphia, Temple University Press.

RICOEUR, P. (1977) *The Rule of Metaphor: Multi-Disciplinary Studies of the Creation of Meaning in Language*, (Trans) CZERNY, R. *et al.*, Toronto, University of Toronto Press.

ROACH, M.E. (1979) 'The social symbolism of women's dress', in CORDWELL, J.M. and SCHWARZ, R.A. (Eds) *The Fabrics of Culture*, The Hague, Paris, New York, Mouton Publishers, pp. 415–22.

ROACH, M.E. and EICHER, J.B. (1973) *The Visible Self: Perspectives on Dress*, Englewood Cliffs, New Jersey, Prentice-Hall.

ROBERTSON, H-J. (1993) *Progress Revisited: The Quality of (Work) Life of Women Teachers*, Ottawa, Ontario, Canadian Teachers' Federation.

ROBERTSON, H-J. (1992) 'Teacher development and gender equity', in HARGREAVES, A. and FULLAN, M.G. (Eds) *Understanding Teacher Development*, New York, Teachers College Press, pp. 43–61.

ROBERTSON, J. (1994) Cinema and the politics of desire in teacher education. (Doctoral dissertation, University of Ottawa, 1994). OISE.

ROSENHOLTZ, S.J. (1989) 'Workplace conditions that affect teacher quality and commitment: Implications for teacher induction programs', *The Elementary School Journal*, 89(4), pp. 421–39.

RUMELHART, D.E. (1980) 'Schemata: The building blocks of cognition', in SPIRO, R.J., BRUCE, B.C. and BREWER, W.F. (Eds) *Theoretical Issues in Reading Comprehension: Perspectives in Cognitive Psychology, Linguistics, and Education*, Hillsdale, NJ, Lawrence Erlbaum Associates, pp. 33–58.

RUSSELL, T. and JOHNSTON, P. (1988) *Teachers Learning from Experiences of Teaching: Analyses Based on Metaphor and Reflection*. Unpublished paper, Faculty of Education, Queen's University, Kingston, Ontario, Canada.

SCHICK, C. (1994) *The University as Text: Women and the University Context*, Halifax, Fernwood Publishing.

SCHOLLE, D. (1991) 'Critical pedagogy and popular culture: The language of critique and possibility', *Journal of Education*, 173(1), pp. 124–137.

SCHÖN, D. (1979) 'Generative metaphor: A perspective on problem-solving in social policy', in ORTONY, A. (Ed) *Metaphor and Thought*, New York, Cambridge University Press, pp. 245–83.

SCHWARTZ, A. (1988) *Annabelle Swift, Kindergartener*, New York, Orchard.

SCHWARTZ, J. (1960) 'The portrayal of educators in motion pictures, 1950–58', *The Journal of Educational Sociology: A Magazine of Theory and Practice*, 34(2), pp. 82–90.

SCHWARZ, R.A. (1979) 'Uncovering the secret vice: Toward an anthropology of clothing and adornment', in CORDWELL, J.M. and SCHWARZ, R.A. *The Fabrics of Culture*, The Hague, Paris, New York, Mouton Publishers, pp. 23–45.

SEITER, E. (1993) *Sold Separately: Parents and Children in Consumer Culture*, New Brunswick, New Jersey, Rutgers University Press.

SKELTON, C. (Ed) (1989) *Whatever Happens to Little Women? Gender and Primary Schooling*, Milton Keynes, Open University Press.

SMITH, N.R. (1972) Developmental origins of graphic symbolization in the paintings of children three to five. Ed.D. Harvard University, Cambridge, MA.

SOLOMON, J. (1988) *Signs of our Times: Semiotics of How to Read Environments and Cultural Objects*, New York, St. Martin's Press.

SPARK, M. (1961) *The Prime of Miss Jean Brodie*, London, Macmillan.

SPRING, J. (1992) *Images of American Life: A History of Ideological Management in Schools, Movies, Radio, and Television*, Albany, NY, SUNY Press.

STERN, S.L. and SCHOENHAUS, T. (1990) *Toyland: The High-Stakes Games of the Toy Industry*, Chicago, Contemporary Books.

STODDARD, M.G. (1991) ' "Kindergarten Cop" — A classroom caper', *The Saturday Evening Post*, Jan/Feb, pp. 58–61.

SUTHERLAND, N. (1992) 'When you listen to the winds of childhood, how much can you believe?', *Curriculum Inquiry*, 22(3), pp. 235–56.

SUZANNE, J. (1992) *Sweet Valley Twins and Friends: Barnyard Battle*, Created by F. PASCAL, New York, Bantam Skylark.

TANNEN, D. (Ed) (1993) *Gender and Conversational Interaction*, New York, Oxford University Press.

TAYLOR, W. (1984) 'Metaphors of educational discourse', in TAYLOR, W. (Ed) *Metaphors of Education*, London, Heinemann Educational Books, pp. 4–19.

TESTER, S.R. (1979) *We Laughed a Lot, My First Day of School*, (Illus) HOOK, F. Chicago, Children's Press.

THORNE, B. (1993) *Gender Play — Girls and Boys in School*, New Brunswick, New Jersey, Rutgers University Press.

TROUSDALE, A.M. (1994) 'Teacher as gatekeeper — Schoolteachers in picture books for young children', in JOSEPH, P.B. and BURNAFORD, G.E. (Eds) *Images of Schoolteachers in Twentieth-Century America — Paragons, Polarities, Complexities*, New York, St. Martin's Press, pp. 195–214.

VAN MANEN, M. (1990) *Researching Lived Experience — Human Science for an Action Sensitive Pedagogy*, London, Ontario, Althouse Press.

WALKERDINE, V. (1990a) 'Sex, power and pedagogy', in WALKERDINE, V. (Ed) *Schoolgirl Fictions*, London, Verso, pp. 1–15.

WALKERDINE, V. (1990b) (Ed) *Schoolgirl Fictions*, London, Verso.

WALLER, W. (1932) *The Sociology of Teaching*, New York, Wiley.

WEBER, S.J. (1990) 'The teacher educator's experience: Generativity and duality of commitment', *Curriculum Inquiry*, 20(2), pp. 141–59.

WEBER, S.J. (1992) 'Playing their way to second-language literacy', *Canadian Children*, 17(1), pp. 51–60.

WEBER, S.J. (1994) *To Sir With Love? Popular Culture as a Conduit to Self-Study*. Paper presented at the annual meeting of the American Educational Research Association, New Orleans, Louisiana, April.

WEBER, S.J. (1993) 'The narrative anecdote in teacher education', *Journal of Education for Teaching*, 19(1), pp. 71–82.

WEBER, S.J. and MITCHELL, C.A. (1993) *Through the Looking Glass: How Children's Views of Teachers and Teaching Can Inform Teacher Education*. International Conference on Teacher Education, Tel-Aviv, Israel, July.

References

WEILER, K. (1988) *Women Teaching for Change: Gender, Class & Power*, New York, Bergin & Garvey.

WEILER, K. (1992) 'Remebering and representing life choices: A critical perspective on teachers' oral history narratives', *Qualitative Studies in Education*, 3(1), pp. 39–50.

WHITE, E.B. (1973) *Stuart Little*, New York, Harper & Row. (First published 1945).

WILLIAMS, C.L. (1989) *Gender Differences at Work: Women and Men in Nontraditional Occupations*, Berkeley, CA, University of California Press.

WILLIAMS, C.L. (1992) 'The glass escalator: Hidden advantages for men in the "female" professions', *Social Problems*, 39(3), pp. 253–64.

WILSON, B. and WILSON, M. (1977) 'An iconoclastic view of the imagery sources in the drawings of young people', *Art Education*, 30(19), pp. 5–11.

WILSON, B. and WILSON, M. (1979) 'Children's story drawings: reinventing worlds', *School Arts*, 78(8), pp. 6–11.

WOLF, N. (1991) *The Beauty Myth: How Images of Beauty Are Used Against Women*, New York, W. Morrow.

WOLFE, T. (1965) 'The secret vice', in *The Kandy-Kolored Tangerine-Flake Streamline Baby*, New York, Farrar, Straus and Giroux, pp. 254–61.

ZANNIS, A. (1994) *Interrogating Feminist Pedagogy in My Classroom: Reflections, Struggles and Challenges.* Unpublished monograph, Faculty of Education, McGill University.

ZEICHNER, K.M. and GRANT, C. (1981) 'Biography and social structure in the socialization of student teachers: A re-examination of the pupil control ideologies of student teachers', *Journal of Education for Teaching*, 3, pp. 299–314.

ZEICHNER, K.M. and TABACHNIK, R.B. (1981) 'Are the effects of university teacher education "washed out" by school experience?', *Journal of Teacher Education*, 32(3), pp. 7–11.

Index

Keene, C. 85
Kelly, T. 102
Kermode, M. 97–8
Kiefer, A. 22
Kinder, M. 74–5
Klein, T. 100
knowledge
  everyday 8
  prior 86
  teachers' 9, 13, 21–2
Knowles, J.G. 5, 9, 21, 65, 131
Koppitz, E.M. 34
Kottkamp, R.B. 21
Kowinski, W.S. 33

Lacey, C. 27, 30
Lakoff, G. 23
Langer, S. 34
Laver, J. 54, 56
Lawton, D. 22
Lepman, J. 20
Lévi-Strauss, C. 56
Lipsitz, G. 26
Liston, D.P. 27, 31
literacy 24, 33, 37
  see cultural studies
    drawing
    text
Lortie, D. 27–8, 130
love
  crushes 109, 117, 120, 122–4, 132
  heterosexual love 109, 119, 135, 136
  same-sex love 109, 122
  teachers' pets 109, 122–4
  see sexuality
Lowenfeld, V. 35
Lurie, A. 55–6, 65, 68, 70, 76, 77
Luttrell, W. 123

Marcel, G. 138
Marshment, M. 95, 120
Masculinity 105, 108
  see gender
    identity
Mason, B.A. 84
maths 18, 43, 48, 50–3, 117
McCloskey, G.N. 21
McCue, H.P. 78
McLaren, A. 44
McNay, M. 103
McNiff, K.K. 35, 40
McRobbie, A. 8, 86, 93, 118, 128
Mead, M. 19, 26–8
Merleau-Ponty, M. 132
metaphor
  analogic 22–3
  conservative 22
  'deep' 23
  hidden 24
  iconic 22–3
  radical 22
  reactionary 22
  root 22–3

'surface' 23
  teaching 27, 32
Miller, C. 118
Miller, J. 76, 101–2, 130, 138
Miller, S.I. 21
Mitchell, C.A. 7, 17, 38–9, 77, 84, 104, 115
Montgomery, L.M. 91, 106
Moonilal-Masur, P. 38
Moore, M. 91–2
Moss, G. 130
movies 2, 4, 7, 10–12, 14, 86, 94, 101, 119–20
Mulvey, L. 120
Munby, H. 21
Musgrave, P.W. 14, 79
myth 3, 8, 31, 38, 47, 130

Nelson, C. 11, 67
non-canonized texts 11, 76–7
  see canonized texts
    fiction
    popular culture
    text

Opie, I. 4
Oram, A. 119

Pascal, F. 1, 78
Payne, C. 47, 49
Peabody, R. 115
Pearson, A.T. 108
pedagogy 3
  activity-based 71, 97
  child-centred 106–8, 113
  experienced-based 82
  high school 48
  of popular culture 11, 128
Penelope, J. 38
Pinar, W. 131
play
  boys' 8, 13, 15, 16, 37–8, 104, 106
  childhood 11, 42
  girls' 5, 10, 37–8, 111, 117, 122, 129
Polan, D. 121
popular culture
  female 10, 38, 46
  male 39
  of childhood 3, 6, 9, 11, 14, 20, 72–6, 85, 109–10, 124, 131
  see cultural imagery
    teachers in popular culture
Provenzo, E.F., Jr. 13, 21, 29, 31, 76, 94, 104
Pullberg, S. 23

Quigly, I. 14, 60, 72, 78–9, 122

Raymond, D. 5, 131
Reid-Walsh, J. 7, 77, 84, 115
Reynolds, K. 4, 5, 14, 77, 103
Roach, M.E. 61, 66
Robertson, H-J. 41, 101
Robertson, J. 3, 6
Robson, M. 22